# RELUCTANT READERS

Connecting students and books for
successful reading experiences

RON JOBE

MARY DAYTON-SAKARI

Pembroke Publishers Limited

©1999   **Pembroke Publishers**
538 Hood Road
Markham, Ontario, Canada L3R 3K9
1-800-997-9807

Distributed in the United States by Stenhouse Publishers
P.O. Box 360
York, Maine 03909
www.stenhouse.com

**Canadian Cataloguing in Publication Data**

Jobe, Ron
    Reluctant readers: connecting students and books for successful reading experiences

Includes bibliographical references
ISBN 1-55138-106-0

1. Reading (Elementary).   2. Children – Books and reading.
I. Sakari, Mary Dayton, 1941 –   .   II. Title.

LB1573.J58 1999              372.4              C98-932984-4

Editor:                Jennifer Drope
Cover Design:          John Zehethofer
Cover Photography:  Ajay Photographics
Typesetting:           JayTee Graphics

Printed and bound in Canada
9 8 7 6 5 4 3 2

# Contents

# Acknowledgements

We would like to express our appreciation to a host of individuals who have shown interest in this book, have given us support and have made useful suggestions.

A special salute must go to the kids in the University of Victoria's reading clinic who, while facing their own struggles to learn to read, gave us so much experience and resulting insight into the process they "endure." In fact, we acknowledge that without them there would be no book.

We are most appreciative of the work of our editor, Jennifer Drope, who was able to see through to the true meaning and organization of the manuscript. Her consistency and focus have added greatly to the integrity of our book. We appreciate her sense of humor, understanding and her ability to listen for what we had really intended.

We are also fortunate to have an "advisory board" of two good friends. We acknowledge and are grateful for the interest, encouragement and direction given to us by our colleague, Paula Hart, who has that rare gift of insightfully identifying murky areas and inconsistencies. She has the talent of being able to verbalize what these are and of clarifying our own feelings of unease. A special thanks too to Sally Clinton who was always there; encouraging, listening, showing interest and reading the final versions for those little unexpected editorial surprises!

We would like to specially recognize Phyllis Simon of Vancouver Kids Books, who played a major consultative role in connection with our resource lists. She and her staff have an amazing grasp of the relevant resources currently intriguing kids. She made countless sugges-

5

tions for books and "cool" areas of interest for us to include. We have also been fortunate to have readily available for consultation, Kelly McKinnon, Sarah Butler, Laurie McNeill and other staff members at Vancouver Kids Books. Our thanks also to Pat and Allen Miller of Storyline Books and the staff of Bolen Books in Victoria for constantly being on the lookout for "hot" books and cross-checking our series lists.

We are appreciative, as well, of the support we received from several outstanding librarians at the Vancouver Public Library: Terry Clark, Mary Eaglesham and Yukio Tosa. We also thank the staff at the Victoria Public Library.

Finally, a word of respect and appreciation to the many educators and kids who have contributed to this book: Colin Chasteauneuf, Russell Collins, Carolyn Cutt, Barb Dean, Jane Doll, Corinne Durston, Margot Filipenko, Matt Filipenko, Jane Flick, April Gill, Don Hamilton, Avis Harley, Joan Perry, Trish Maskell, John Naslund, Jo-Anne Naslund, Patricia Shields, Sandy Shook, Elizabeth Smith, Mercedes Smith, Jennette Stark, Carolyn Varah, Joan Weir and Myrna Ziola.

# Foreword * Reluctantly Yours!

*Reluctance is not unique to reluctant readers.*

As you read this book, be aware that we are influenced by a concern for kids who don't find reading easy or enjoyable, our reluctant readers, and a realization that everyone faces being reluctant about something. Yes, most of us are indeed members of the "Procrastinator's Club," and we might as well recognize it!

Just as some kids are afraid of and avoid reading and are successful in devising their own avoidance strategies, so are all procrastinators. Probably you'll have no trouble in identifying an unpleasant task you don't want to do. For Ron, it's ironing. He'll do anything to avoid it—telephone a friend, dust, create distractions and even convince himself that nobody will notice his creased pants. Mary, on the other hand, hates to arrive home, stare in the fridge and know that she has to come up with something—anything—for supper. She puts off the decision as long as her hunger pangs allow; reading the paper, drinking tea, washing the counters, feeding the dogs and pulling weeds. Think of your own reluctance in facing a task and you will feel what a reluctant reader feels about reading.

Writing a letter is another activity that brings out everybody's reluctance. The terror of looking at a blank page is too much for many of us—so we avoid the experience. Perhaps the pencil is dull, so it has to be sharpened, eh? This could lead to cleaning the entire desk top off or sorting a drawer or two. By then, with any luck, time is up.

Starting to read a book, even for habitual readers, can result in the same avoidance strategies. What excuses have you used for not reading a book recently, especially the "ones" that are constantly reminding you of its presence? "I'm too busy! I'm a slow reader! I'll read it before I go to bed." But, when you get there, it's too often, "I'm too tired! It looks too thick and the cover is boring. I'll find time tomorrow!"

*We never "find time" to read...*

*...we must "make time" to read!*

This statement is true for all of us. We "must" make time to read. "How?" is the big question. Look at your daily schedule and ask yourself if you are presently making time to read. Can you get up earlier or go to bed later? Can you read on the way to work? Can you set a special time, say right after supper, to read?

In the classroom, making time to read works the same way. Students have to have time to read. Do you provide for an uninterrupted silent reading time? A reading break? Do you read aloud regularly to the class? Do you tell stories? Do you insist that your students always have a book with them to read when they finish their work? Do you read the books they are reading? If you answer any questions with a "no," you, or your students, may be in danger of becoming self-designated non-readers.

With so many teachers, teacher-librarians and parents being self-designated non-readers themselves, is it any surprise that kids are too? Surely the existence of self-designated non-readers gives a new meaning to the word literacy. Is just being able to sound out the words enough in our society? Literacy is being able to comprehend meaning, to detect bias and to ferret out innuendo or implications. It would seem then that even if a reader can comprehend but chooses not to read, that too is non-reading—it's called aliteracy.

This book is dedicated to teachers and parents of reluctant readers who have hit the wall in their frustrated attempts to help and need a new approach. Our aim is to offer a new way of looking at the situation and new suggestions for those who work with youngsters in grades three to six who are reading below grade level.

## Using This Book

Our objective in writing this book is to clarify the world of reluctant readers, show how they are caught because of their beliefs and suggest ways for you to help them get beyond their barriers. Always the focus is on how to encourage self-designated non-readers to become life-long, competent readers. In this book, we show how literature can be used to hook reluctant readers into the wealth of ideas, humor and information contained in books, and, above all, the delight of a good read. A love of reading is the greatest gift a parent or teacher can give to a child.

Chapter 1, "The Challenge of Reading," considers why kids read or do not read. In a variety of classrooms kids frankly shared their thoughts on this topic with us. We also try to indicate in this chapter what we feel is the power of literature in everyone's lives.

Chapter 2, "Who Are the Reluctant Readers?," offers a categorization of these readers according to their own views of themselves, which reflect their realities and beliefs about reading. Beginning with this chapter we have purposely highlighted the characteristics of each type of reluctant reader along with stories of real children. We have selectively included resources and strategies to facilitate success with each type of reader.

Chapter 3, "How to Get Rid of Reader Reluctance," realistically assesses the influences on these children both from internal and external forces. We have purposely tried to overcome the constant repetition of the same old skill-focused approach. We believe that for success to occur with these youngsters, you have to blindside them. In other words, you change your direction of instruction or behavioral patterns and catch them off guard.

Chapter 4, "User-Friendly Entry Points for Reluctant Readers," presents a wide range of resources that can successfully be used with reluctant readers. We know they like these books; they've told us so. We've included an extensive spectrum of available books; from wordless to alphabet, to chapter books and beyond, but they should only be viewed as a sampling of the many possibilities available. Not everything will work with every kid—you have to pick and choose. Another important point in this chapter is that teachers have to stop being so serious and remember how to play, particularly with language.

Chapter 5, "Go with the Kids! Interest Entry Points," offers numerous topics that reluctant readers have come up with over and over. We have purposely kept the sections brief, as our intent is to show a variety of possible starting points. These include lots of titles and a bevy of authors to explore further.

The conclusion, "Secrets to Success with Reluctant Readers," summarizes the key points we would like you to remember.

Finally, complete author and title references for all titles mentioned throughout the book are found in the bibliography at the end of the book.

We have also used the following markers to highlight the major points and links we are trying to make throughout the book:

> **Reflections:**
> Placed strategically throughout the book, these encourage teachers and parents to think about the issues and strategies essential with reluctant kids.

*KidLinks:*

These are strategies designed to appeal to reluctant readers. They are planned to suggest, stimulate and point out new directions.

*AuthorLinks:*

The works of many authors are appropriate for reluctant readers, yet certain authors seem to be better able to capture the imagination. We feature some of these writers along with some of their titles. Each link is only a brief glimpse, but the sections serve to entice teachers and parents to locate more books by these individuals.

*ComputerLinks:*

There can be no doubt whatsoever that computers are an important tool in every classroom and home. Strategies and resources for using computers directly are referred to in each of these sections.

*ResearchLinks:*

Much has been accomplished in the research on reading, reluctance, motivation and children's literature. Each link is designed to remind the teacher of a specific research finding that has relevance for working with reluctant readers.

*Bibliographies:*

Books, books, books. These are not meant to be all-inclusive listings but rather, selective guides to offer new directions for exploration in various media. Who knows where the interests of reluctant readers will take you? As a teacher or parent you're about to learn a great deal more than you bargained for, will enjoy more stories than you could have thought possible and will celebrate laughter as you move forward taking the reluctant readers with you.

# 1 * The Challenge of Reading

*More people read today than have ever read before.*

Media alarmists try to tell us that our entire culture is becoming more illiterate—that more children are reading below grade level and that every year schools are doing a worse job.

Despite the many reluctant readers we work with, research does not sustain this view.

There are as many ways of reading as there are materials to read—not just books, but computer screens, magazines, signs, manuals, comics and illustrations. We read in a different way now. Just as our eating habits have changed over the past decade and now we often graze rather than have three set meals per day, so too have our reading habits changed. These days, many people prefer to sample newspapers, magazines, listserves or Web pages, rather than tackle big chunks of print.

Similarly, children's books have changed dramatically. One can note this in the explosion of highly visual information books filled with detailed illustrations and photographs. The look of the text has changed too—often written in short snippets and appearing in varying type faces and sizes. Children's novels also reflect this graphic evolution as publishers attempt to make them more user-friendly. Thus, we see an increase in illustrations, even more white space, larger print and a move toward color illustrations.

This trend of both readers and publishers moving toward materials that can easily be browsed and smaller snippets of text is perhaps a reflection of our culture's current desire to do everything faster than fast! This does not mean, however, that people do not know how to read; they are perhaps just more selective about how they do it.

## Why Read?

If you ask kids why they read, they will tell you they read to:

- find out things;
- discover how to do something;
- have new experiences, especially frightening ones, safely;
- experience excitement and adventure;
- escape.

## Why Don't We Read?

Even though there are many good reasons to read, we simply don't. Why? If you ask kids why they don't read, they'll say:

- I'm a slow reader.
- I'm too busy.
- Only girls read! I'd rather play basketball.
- It's boring.
- It's easier to watch a video or TV.

*I'm a slow reader* —This is a common perception heard from everyone, kids and adults. Why? Because we have learned one reading speed. We frequently read everything as if it was a physics text! Somehow we did not get the message that what we really need to be is a "flexible and inferential reader."

We agree that there is a time and place for all things—for example, time to read slowly to savor the language or to reread favorite passages—but if we are in the midst of a high-action part of a novel and the author is helping us by giving us short, rapidly-paced sentences for the dialogue or narration, it behooves us to move more quickly. It simply adds to our enjoyment. When it is an information book, we need to be able to graze or browse just as well as concentrate word for word. Don't forget that flexibility also refers to varying the types of materials we read.

*I'm too busy*—Kids have too many scheduled events and too many places to go in their daily lives. Adults have too much to do, therefore they have to find ways of keeping the kids busy. Activities fill up time when parents can't be there. If kids get to do a lot, it is supposed to be quality time. What today's children don't get is the time to be on their own, to be inventive or contemplative, to use their imaginations and to be creative. They need a break. Reading can become a way of having quiet time to escape from the pressures of reality and let the forces of their imagination roam. Otherwise they can be caught in the web of immediacy—reading only cereal boxes, candy wrappers and mindless computer games. Thus another aliterate is developed.

*Only girls read! I'd rather play basketball*—A common gender stereotyping is that boys don't read and don't need to read because they are action creatures! This is why, for their emotional and intellectual development, it is particularly important for boys to have men as reading models, especially to see dad/uncle/grandpa read, laugh, cry and wonder. It is important for boys to see how men value and question the printed word. Just because it is written does not mean it is correct or accurate. Men need to allow children's viewpoints to be heard and respected if critical, creative minds are to be developed.

There is a time for sharing the joy of tears, as in *Charlotte's Web* when Charlotte the spider dies. "Real" men need not avoid death and other trying issues in the literature, but instead should share these accounts to help give their boys an emotional schema on which to rely. In other words, to experience emotion in fiction helps people prepare for facing similar events in their own lives. Children can take heed of a small action in Judith Viorst's *The 10th Good Thing About Barney*. In this book, when a young boy's beloved cat dies, he makes a list of ten wonderful things to remember about his pet.

## Why Literature for Reluctant Readers?

We read to find out who we are and to enrich our lives. Literature is a humanizing force that allows us to get in touch with our senses, feelings and emotions. Through reading, we extend our own backgrounds and are enabled to vicariously experience, feel and recognize the thoughts and emotions of others. Thus, we gradually learn to understand feelings of love, joy, dislike or distrust. There is a tremendous sense of joy and relief when reading a book to discover, "I'm not the only one!" The characters become alive as we read and share their problems, dilemmas and emotional conflicts.

Reading good books makes us think as we question the thoughts and actions of a character. "Why did he do that? Why didn't she say this? If only he had come right out and said how he felt." We develop our own sense of right and wrong as we reflect on a character's actions. For example, was Marty in *Shiloh* right in not telling his parents that he had hidden the lost dog?

As Ron Jobe points out in his book, *Cultural Connections,* literature allows us to see our own culture and to experience the culture of others in a way we cannot do in our daily life. It is important that kids of all cultural heritages see themselves reflected in the books they read, especially given the multicultural reality of the classrooms in our country.

For many adults and children, literature also provides one of the most enjoyable means to escape from our ordinary lives. One moment we can be with Shabanu on the hot Pakistan desert in *Shabanu: Daughter of the Wind,* another with Julie on the arctic tundra surviving with a wolf pack in *Julie of the Wolves,* and another with Brian in the Ontario wilderness after the plane crash in *Hatchet.* In a twinkling of an eye we can zip back to prehistoric times to explore the medieval world of Birdy in *Catherine Called Birdy* or "teseract" to the future world with Charles Wallace in *Wrinkle in Time,* Olwen in *The Keeper of the Isis Light* or Jonas in *The Giver.*

Another major benefit of literature is its ability to stimulate our aesthetic awareness of the beauty of language and style. Quality selections provide us with models of literary language; sometimes they will be the only standard English many children will hear. Simplicity in language is hard to achieve, but Patricia MacLachlan in *Sarah, Plain and Tall* shows just how much can be told by using terse poetic language. Still other books, such as Bill Peet's amusing *Big Bad Bruce* and *The Caboose Who Got Loose,* are loaded with wit and a sense of fun with language.

Perhaps one of the most important reasons why we should share more literature with reluctant readers is that it is a main source for the development of their imaginations. We all need to wonder and dream about life. To speculate what would happen if...? To dream of other worlds. To enter into the world of the characters and actively delve into the issues affecting them.

For reluctant readers, the power of literature is that it brings them out of themselves. Content and language use give them something to focus on besides their anxiety over not being able to read. With really good books, fiction and information, these readers forget to believe that they can't read.

Let us not forget that for all of us, literature makes us think, ponder, wonder and imagine. Our lives are enriched and we feel a sense of fulfillment and pleasure when we are involved in a good book. It is no different for reluctant readers; they just haven't had the same access.

## Why Should Adults Read to Kids?

As adults, we underestimate the significance of being models of behavior for children. This is particularly true when it comes to reading. Children need to see that reading is an important part of life. If an adult is seen reading regularly, then it is! If not, it isn't! To be good models of literacy, we must go beyond the act of reading and discuss what we are reading with our kids. Discussion is a way into meaning, and comprehending meaning is what reading is all about.

Books should be shared aloud with all kids, both in the home and in the classroom. As responses are shared, questions are asked. Questions, particularly inferential questions, are what get at meaning. "Why did a character do a specific action? Why did the author give us a hint and then nothing happened? What is going to happen next? Why?" It is important to remember that a good story is a good story for all ages.

In a family with varying age groups, it is typical to encounter a variety of reading materials with many levels of readability, from newspapers, magazines and cookbooks, to picture books, novels, poetry and classics. These may be in two or more languages if parents or grandparents who speak another language are present—a further enrichment of the reading experience.

Being a mature reader means that we sometimes read from serious tomes and books of information, but over the holidays how many of us have a trashy novel to resort to as escapist reading? We love it ... as it gets us away from life around us, especially if we add romance and a palm tree or two. Adults read just for fun too!

This is well known to all of us, but somehow we forget the enjoyment part when we work with reluctant readers. All too often they face a "skills-orientated" program, which, because it is not real reading, turns them off and makes them ignore the exercise as they do it. When they fall behind or choose to follow a different drummer, our answer is too often more skills. We need to ask ourselves, "If we had put more emphasis on reading for enjoyment instead of worksheets, wouldn't they be more positive about reading?"

# 2 * Who Are the Reluctant Readers?

*Reluctant readers are not born, they are made.*

Struggling readers are not blank slates. They have the knowledge they need to become competent readers; they just do not use it. Years of special assistance and instruction have exposed them to all the skills necessary for reading. They use phonics: usually getting half the letters and sounds in a word right and using beginning and ending sounds. They use context: getting the general meaning of what they are reading and often retelling some details. They use vocabulary: connecting the right meaning for homophones and choosing the correct spelling for the meaning. The problem is not lack of skills, but failing to use the skills they have. Reluctant readers don't believe they can!

They see themselves as non-readers and believe they cannot read at all. These individuals believe they will always fail and that they cannot succeed no matter what they do. They have become discouraged, yet, they have the potential to become good readers. We can help by recognizing their negative beliefs and guiding them to get beyond their negativity, to do the work required to learn and to actually practice the tasks of reading and writing.

Reluctant readers fall into several recognizable groups based on what they believe about themselves. We have labeled these groups as follows:

- "I can't,"
- "I don't know how,"

- "I'd rather" and
- "I don't care" readers.

There are also two other groups of readers who struggle but whom we do not consider to be true "reluctant" readers: the English as a Second Language (ESL) readers and the very small group of children with physical or mental disabilities that prevent them from learning. We have included suggestions for them as well.

## "I Can't" Readers

**Characteristics:**

- Passive;
- Avoidance experts;
- Afraid to take risks.

"I can't" readers come in two versions, those that act out and those that hide out.

*Carla*—One such acting out "I can't" reader is Carla. In constant motion, she cannot sit or stand still. For her, sitting still begins with arms up over her head, head flung back, feet hitting the underside of the table; then arms are spread across the table, head is balanced sideways on one arm—eyes away from the book— and legs are wrapped around the legs of the chair; next, feet are upon the chair, arms are hugging her legs and forehead is down on her knees; and on and on. Standing still is: moving to the window to look out; inspecting carved initials on the desk; picking up a piece of eraser from the floor; and then fumbling with a pencil, then a sheet of paper, then the book. And all of this when she says she is "being still."

Carla's answers are strident and loud. She is argumentative and finds fault in others. According to Carla, all her problems are someone else's fault. Carla has many difficulties with reading but the biggest is that she is "afraid to try, afraid to fail." Some would describe Carla as a child with ADHD (attention deficit hyperactive disorder) and many children like her have been so labeled.

*Darrin*—While Carla acts out, Darrin hides out. He has the same "I can't" stance toward reading, but reacts passively instead of actively. Darrin sits still, stands still, in fact is so still that he fades into the background. He slumps in his chair, head down, fiddling with an eraser under his desk. Very compliant, when asked to, he will sit up, open the book, hold it up, even look at it, but he isn't reading; he is just obeying.

While writing, Darrin never gets beyond erasing each and every word he writes. His mind is blank.

For him, Carla and other children like them, the biggest difficulty is their perfectionist fear of failure. Their solution is if I don't try, I won't fail. "I can't" readers are afraid to be wrong and afraid of getting corrected. Overactivity or passivity is their defense.

**Resources to Facilitate Success:**
- Interactive, physical action books;
- Reading games that demand movement;
- Computer programs and games;
- "Any book that catches their interest."

**Strategies to Facilitate Success:**
- Integrate physical, kinetic movement through such activities as:
  —role-playing a character in a book;
  —copying a text;
  —playing reading games that demand movement;
  —learning computer skills and word processing.
- Provide quick successes through small risks and small choices, including:
  —using CD-ROM programs or searching the Web;
  —choosing words to write in lists.
- Provide activities with no wrong answers where any answer is right, for example:
  —building sentences in the style shown in Bill Martin, Jr.'s *Sounds of Language* reading series by adding descriptive words to a simple sentence or by substituting more specific words for general verbs, nouns, adverbs or adjectives;
  —making lists of possibilities.
- Normalize mistakes. This is aided when teachers are seen discussing their mistakes and miscues.

---

*Reflection:*
"I can't" readers benefit from any strategy that demands movement. For overactive children like Carla, these strategies direct their movement toward a specific focus and in so doing eliminate their random, unproductive movement. For passive children like Darrin, strategies that demand manipulation get them physically moving and also force them to focus and engage their minds on the reading activity.

---

In each of the following sections, the activities are devised to show how an idea can be adapted first for an individual then for class groupings. This particular strategy uses movement and action to get the students physically involved with literacy. The success of these strategies for an "I can't" reader is in getting them up out of their chair, moving around, involved and interested.

### SPY TRAINING

This activity is based on Louise Fitzhugh's *Harriet, the Spy*, an account of a girl's effort to find out the facts about several people. Issue the students with the proper equipment to become spies: writing pads, pens and unobtrusive clothing. A baseball cap with a visor to shade the eyes from suspicious viewers is a must. Decide on a location that would be good to observe people—a mall, library or a busy street corner might work. Establish a good "blind" from which to observe without being detected. For example, one could lurk outside a small specialty shop (e.g. one selling chocolates or vegetables), observing people who frequent it and writing notes about what is seen.

### MASTER DETECTIVES

In the classroom, Harriet could give way to an activity based on Donald Sobol's *Encyclopedia Brown*. To begin, set up small group "Detective Agencies." Ask each agency to create or invent for the students a mysterious situation based on a case facing Encyclopedia Brown. To solve the mystery, each group is required to go out into the school playground or the local community to observe the situation. Each "agency" then tries to solve the mystery through discussing the notes they have taken while watching. The different solutions can be compared and defended. Other books that could be shared in such a fashion include Charles Townsend's *World's Most Baffling Puzzles* and Ken Weber's *The Five-Minute Mysteries*. This is a lead into reading mysteries such as those involving Nancy Drew, the Hardy Boys or Eric Wilson's detectives.

## "I Don't Know How" Readers

**Characteristics:**
- Easily frustrated;
- Reliant on the teacher;
- Not responsible;
- Frequently absent from instruction.

Somehow "I don't know how" readers seem to have empty minds when it comes to reading.

*James*—Being just such a child, James became an "I don't know how" reader because of a continuing ear and sinus infection that means he is often absent from school. Between missing so much instruction and his poor hearing, it is hard for him to attend to what is going on at the front of the room. He gets to the point where all is noise and to cope he tunes everything, even instruction, out.

James has no commitment to reading, viewing it as school "work" laid on by others. He would rather use what is being read as a jumping off place for discussion. He can connect almost any book he is supposed to try to read to his interest—farming. Then, off he goes on this topic and through his chat he takes the teacher right along with him. James endures and avoids reading instruction instead of practicing reading. He has only one resource for help with reading and it is not phonics, context, or even pictures. He just looks to his teacher, expecting her to give him the answer. And falling into the trap, she does.

Somehow readers like James do not realize that they, just like everyone else, must do the mental work involved in any learning and that everyone starts with nothing and gets more proficient by trying. This belief is made worse because these readers often miss school through illness or by moving from school to school and so, receive reading instruction only in isolated dribs and drabs, to which they pay no attention.

### Resources to Facilitate Success:
- High-interest, low-vocabulary materials;
- Wordless books;
- Pattern and alliteration books;
- "Any book that catches their interest."

### Strategies to Facilitate Success:
- Encourage decision-making; giving choices stimulates mental involvement.
- Promote metacognitive understanding behind decisions as recommended by Sandra McCormick in her book *Instructing Students Who have Literacy Problems.* This might include:
  —discussing the "why" of choosing "this" rather than "that," before, during and after reading;
  —using planning to find purpose and to distinguish important from non-important details;
  —monitoring to know when we understand or not;

—correcting misunderstandings.
- Offer language experience activities that provide connections from reading to writing.
- Introduce reading games that demand mental activity.

---

*Reflection:*

James and others like him would benefit from strategies that engage their minds: ones that demand thought and require decision making, mental focus and attention. "I don't know how" readers like to talk. We need to direct this willingness to talk toward discussing the process of reading rather than the content of the story. Reluctant readers must become aware of what we all do when we read. Only when they realize that reading must be worked at and not just absorbed will improvement begin.

---

### KidLink: Mad on Games

We all have favorite board games. Reluctant readers do too. Part of a board game's appeal is that it involves a pattern to find, think through and solve. The following activities are part of a strategy that mentally involves kids in books, but also gives them an outlet for their energy and need for action.

#### PLAY IT AGAIN, SAM!

What would a particular game be like if it were also based on a favorite book? Get your reader to choose a favorite story (e.g. plot, character, setting), genre (e.g. mystery, choose your own adventure, fantasy) or content (e.g. marine life, Star Wars, motorcycles, baseball) as the topic for a new game that will be based on one they know. Ask the reader to mentally lay out the new game, create a board pattern, write new rules and new directions, and produce new game cards. Finally, have the reader try the game out on someone and then edit. By recreating a game, the reluctant reader is thinking through, discussing and making decisions about how to make it viable and how it must proceed. He or she is engaged in organizing, writing and reading. Sid Sackson's *The Book of Classic Board Games* includes 15 different board games that can be used as starting points.

#### CHANGING PATTERNS

In the classroom, ask kids to work in pairs to adapt the pattern ideas and formats from commercially prepared materials such as card games, sports or author cards, pop-up books or cartoons to create their own

21

new versions. The idea is to reuse the format to relate to long-standing interests or current science or social studies content. This type of re-creation is along the lines of beginning readers recreating pattern books such as Bill Martin, Jr.'s *Brown Bear, Brown Bear*, but at a much more intellectually complex level.

## "I'd Rather" Readers

**Characteristics:**
- Thing-oriented;
- Hands on;
- Interested in the world;
- Good at crafts and art.

"I'd rather" readers are information seekers. Usually they are very active and like finding out about the real world.

*Matthew*—Mad about motorcycles, he easily lectures his teacher on V-twin, vertical-twin, or opposed-twin two-cycle versus four-cycle engines; torque; horsepower; "hogs" versus dirt machines; and the virtues of overhead cams, fuel injection and nobbies. Matthew will not even attempt a book unless it is full of pictures of motorcycles. He devours motorcycle magazines and brochures. When his teacher finally caved in and brought his own motorcycle to school, the two of them read and wrote outside next to the bike. On any other subject or story his attention constantly strays, his hand doodles tires, frames and exhaust flames and his mind is obviously gearing down some bike trail. What works best in keeping him focused on literacy is the "beginners motorcycle manual" they are creating together.

Schools often fail these "I'd rather" readers. Readers like Matthew are almost exclusively focused on only one topic, in his case motorcycles, and schools do not allow for such concentration. Nothing but their one topic interests such students and nothing else may interest them for their whole lives. They often do not see the value of reading or writing and the only way to change that is through using their particular interest as the topic of literacy. After a while they begin to see that there is a point to learning to read; that by knowing how to read, they can delve deeper and more completely into their favorite subject.

**Resources to Facilitate Success:**
- How-to books;
- Interactive books;

- Non-fiction books;
- "Any book that catches their interest."

**Strategies to Facilitate Success:**
- Give choice.
- Provide thought-provoking objects that can be investigated more thoroughly through books as does Christine Pappas in *An Integrated Language Perspective in the Elementary School*.
- Introduce a book by presenting several objects that represent important aspects in the story.
- Focus on materials from the "real world."

---

*Reflection:*

Matthew and other "I'd rather" reluctant readers would benefit from strategies that allow for concentration on their particular interest and manipulation of artifacts related to that interest. Reading and writing can then be slipped in as tools for digging out more information.

---

*KidLink: Guess What's "Cool" Today!*

Any aspect of any interest can turn into a project. Projects draw out literacy skills and get students emotionally involved through their interests.

*DOODLING A DOODLE*

All kids like to doodle! Catch them at it, doodling curly letters down the margin of every page, and you have a chance to start a fascinating conversation about "fancy writing" and "picture letters." This could lead to a small investigation of calligraphy, illustrated scripts, how ink was developed, pre-Roman letters, secret codes, newspapers, computer fonts or other aspects of writing. A valuable resource for this type of project is a mock newspaper from another time, such as those in Rachel Wright's *The Viking News*, with its mention of the runes. Kids will be fascinated by *The History of Making Books* in the Scholastic Voyages of Discovery series, with its exciting formatting using see-through views, flaps, high-gloss finish and lots of references. Peter Grislis's *The Calligraphy Book* is a graphic how-to book.

*WILDLIFE ALERT*

Are there coyotes just over your back fence? In most cities, skunks, raccoons and even coyotes are on the rise. Some communities might even have deer, bears or cougars as visitors. Are crows taking over your community? Intrigue the students by challenging them to ask their parents and neighbors about any wild critters seen in their area. Who has seen them? Local wildlife agencies, the public library and local newspaper articles may be helpful. Creating charts of different animals with information on how many sightings, city habitats, safety issues or trails they travel offer opportunities to categorize what they find out. Naturally, highly visual books need to be consulted for the facts. Consider using Diane Swanson's *Coyotes in the Crosswalk: Canadian Wildlife in the City* to get intrigued or Jean Craighead George's *The Cry of the Crow* to gain insight into the communication abilities of these noise makers.

## "I Don't Care" Readers

**Characteristics:**
- Disinterested or bored;
- Habitual failures;
- Expert at coping skills;
- Usually older readers.

"I don't care" readers have failed for so long they deny they can or even want to succeed at literacy.

*Justine*—Glorifying the life of a street kid and having tried it out by pan handling with her dog on summer days, Justine at twelve maintains that school has nothing to offer her—that school isn't in the real world and doesn't provide what she needs. Nor does she see any need for reading and writing. Even though she reads at about a grade three level, she says she can read as much as she needs and she can get by. She doesn't like "story books" because, according to Justine, you can go see the movie or watch it on television. These are better because you can see it. Without realizing that with her current literacy ability, the best she can hope for is some sort of minimum wage job, she thinks she would make a good lawyer or maybe a social worker. She would like to help street people and those jobs would be good for that.

Justine's understandings and expectations of life don't match. Although she doesn't value literacy, she needs it desperately to be able to have any life at all above the poverty line. Justine and other reluctant readers like her don't realize that literacy is the economic survival skill it is in our culture.

**Resources to Facilitate Success:**
- "Cool" books and comics;
- Peer recommended materials, pop music, raps;
- Computers and the Web;
- "Real life" materials—job applications, license manuals, forms;
- "Any book that catches their interest."

**Strategies to Facilitate Success:**
- Encourage projects that relate to future success.
- Teach word processing and Web search skills.
- Create graphic organizers.
- Concentrate on researching the "how to" of studying a topic by focusing on locating, organizing and presenting as suggested in Charles Temple and Jean Gillet's book *Language and Literacy*.

---

*Reflection:*
Effective strategies must be based on "real life" interests such as finding a job to capture the interest of a reader with an "I don't care" attitude.

---

*KidLink: Get a Life!*
The following activities highlight a strategy that uses the skills necessary for creating a report: locating, sorting, classifying, organizing and presenting information.

*HELP THAT DOG!*

All that is needed for this activity is a reader who sees something that needs to be put right or a job they want to know more about, and an organization that encourages volunteers. One such reader became very incensed over a stray dog destruction story on the local television station. During a discussion, her teacher mentioned the work the Society for the Prevention of Cruelty to Animals (SPCA) does with abandoned animals. The student was intrigued and they set up a visit (the reader found the number in the phone book, made the call and the appointment, etc.). When they arrived, a volunteer gave them a tour and brochures, and talked about their various volunteer programs. The reader was particularly interested in the Junior SPCA Program open to children aged 6 to 16. She read the handout, filled out the form, went to the meetings and got to help out topping up water dishes and straightening pet beds. One resource worth checking out for this topic is

*Puppy: A Practical Guide to Caring for Your Puppy,* one in a series of SPCA pet care guides.

The previous strategy could easily be extended to a classroom setting. Since it is built on individual angst and interest, each reader's topic will probably be different. But the "how to" of setting up visits, researching a topic, getting speakers, creating a poster report, etc., could be done as a class. Possible topics to interest them might include the truth about cigarette smoking, the facts about drug use, finding a summer job, the realities of hitchhiking or even building a bike with little money.

## "What? I Don't Understand!" Readers

**Characteristics:**
- Lack vocabulary, not concepts;
- Lack cultural meaning.

English as a Second Language (ESL) students are a group outside the major theme of this book, yet a few words about their struggle would not be amiss.

*Oliver*—Speaking Cantonese in his home, Oliver did not start learning English until entering preschool at age four. He started feeling some confidence in his English ability about halfway through grade one. Oliver is a quiet and shy boy until he gets to know you. Then he shows enormous curiosity and every question is a "why" question. When it comes to reading itself, he enjoys hearing stories read by others but balks at reading aloud. He is still unsure of some of the letter sounds and really hesitates at sounding them out. When faced with a word he doesn't know or with explaining the meaning of an idea in a book, he just says, "I don't know." His "I don't know" strategy is more a reflection of his lack of self-confidence in his ability than a reflection of not knowing. What he really means is, "I don't feel confident that I have the words to express it."

ESL kids bring meaning and schemata from their experience and their first language. Their struggle is in joining the concepts and the literacy skills they have to the sounds and the meanings of a new language—its melody, structure, organization and vocabulary.

**Resources to Facilitate Success:**
- Picture dictionaries with illustrations and labels;
- Graphic information books;

- Sophisticated alphabet books;
- "Any book that catches their interest."

**Strategies to Facilitate Success:**
- Share culturally connected stories, jokes, ads and ideas.
- Cultivate word play.
- Annotate diagrams and posters.
- Promote understanding of key visuals such as graphs, maps, flow charts, etc., as visual summaries of informational text content as reported in Margaret Early's article, "Using key visuals to aid ESL students' text comprehension."
- Engage in choral reading and reader's theatre.
- Use predictable pattern books.

---

*Reflection:*

Oliver and other ESL students would benefit from any literacy strategy that develops their oral competence and extends their vocabulary. Instruction should not only increase the number of words they can understand but also the number of meanings for each word.

---

#### KidLink: Words Give the Message
The activities that follow are based on a strategy that uses the idea of modeling to help show the rhythm, tempo and melody of the language as well as begin to try different vocal interpretations to clarify meaning.

*THE BARE/BEAR FACTS*

The English language is filled with double meanings as in the word "fair", vague cultural references like "cool" or "awesome", expressions such as "you know" and homonyms that get in the way of communication. Ask reluctant readers to find sentences, phrases or words that could be interpreted in more than one way or that have different shades of meaning depending on the emphasis. They can then do non-verbal interpretive movements to express the different meanings. Enjoy Peggy Parish's *Amelia Bedelia* or Fred Gwynne's *Chocolate Moose for Dinner.*

*SIMON SAYS, SIMON REPEATS*

Based on the old childhood game, say to the students: "Simon says ...." Instead of an action (i.e. take two steps forward/backward, etc.), give a line of a poem or book. The students then say it back to you in unison, reflecting your vocal expression. This game could also be done with the students being out if the teacher says something wrong and they repeat it. This makes for much laughter and good spirits.

## The Real "I Have a Reading Problem" Readers

**Characteristics:**
- Specific physical or mental disabilities;
- Inability to use language effectively;
- Possible visual or hearing difficulties.

It must be acknowledged that some children may be deterred from learning to read because of very real physical problems that affect their sight, their hearing or their brain. Most authorities agree that they are a very small percentage of struggling readers, perhaps only 3% of the total school-age population.

*John* — A happy, interested 11 year old, John is keen to learn to read. He is in a special education classroom and functioning well below his grade level. John's speech is immature for his age and his pronunciation unclear. He can read grade one books, but even then needs help. He reads word-by-word and understands what he reads in a general way, although he doesn't pay much attention to details and fails to see the relationships inherent in all stories. His printing is beautiful but his spelling is based on letter names and sounds and is dependent on the first letter. Writing a meaningful sentence is a difficult process. John is reading, and his reading may develop somewhat further over time, but he is one of those few who are already working at their potential.

John and other children with language disabilities have difficulty in applying thinking processes not just to reading but to other types of learning as well. They often never reach an emergent reading level.

**Resources to Facilitate Success:**
- Predictable pattern books;
- Computer programs with voice;
- Wordless picture books;
- Taped books;
- "Any book that catches their interest."

**Strategies to Facilitate Success:**
- Undertake language experience.
- Practice writing and "copy writing."

- Investigate environmental print.
- Build word banks.
- Make time for shared book experiences and allowing the kids to track and share the reading as you read aloud as in Don Holdaway's book *The Foundations of Literacy*.
- Practice echo reading.

---

*Reflection:*

The strategies suggested throughout this book certainly will not harm these disabled readers and probably do more good than a skill-and-drill approach. Just as with reluctant readers, catching their attention and their interest is paramount. Any topic, process or material presented here can be adapted to their ability level.

---

## KidLink: Tape Your Talk

The following activities are based on a strategy that uses listening to make the connection to reading and writing. This strategy has the potential for sustaining interested, repeated practice.

### WALKMAN WALKABOUT

Taped books and stories are "cool" with students, especially the older ones. They can have their walkmans on and nobody knows what they are listening to. Previously recorded magazine articles, car manuals, etc., can be incentives to tackle printed materials at their age level. Make a grand collection of tapes of articles and stories and allow the students to listen to them in class. These students can "look at" the written version of the book at the time they are listening to it — an extension of the listening centre.

### THE WEEKLY RADIO

To extend this activity, children can create a weekly news tape and newspaper that includes things that happened in the school or community, good things students were seen doing at break time, excerpts from novels, information books or magazines, jokes, riddles, etc., for all in the class, but especially these really disabled readers.

# 3 * How to Get Rid of Reader Reluctance

*What you believe is what you get!*

There are as many ways to create reluctant readers as there are reluctant kids. Reluctant readers are just as individual and have as many differences as any other readers. All have different background knowledge depending on their life experiences. This includes their knowledge of how to read and their approach to avoiding learning. Yet, the same sorts of internal and external stumbling blocks inhibit them all.

Some internal inhibitors include:
* the beliefs kids hold about their abilities;
* the types of interests kids enjoy;
* their lack of control over reading.

Some external inhibitors include:
* the pressures of time and curriculum;
* the teacher's patience;
* the level of the teacher's awareness;
* the weak modeling kids may have received.

Reluctant readers are afraid of literacy—afraid of attempting to read and write. Their whole belief system says they never could, can't now and never will read; so they say "I can't," "I don't know how," "I'd rather not" or "I don't care." They have given up. With these readers, our task goes beyond instructing in word identification or comprehension. Actually, they will never be willing to attempt to learn reading skills unless we help them change the way they feel about reading. Our task is to bring these kids to the point where they realize they can read, and we have to do it without them being aware they are actually reading and learning. The secret is to make instruction look like it isn't instruction. It must appear to reluctant readers that the point of what they are doing is just for fun or for finding out something they want to know. They must feel that the point is not to practice the skills of reading.

With these children, the best way to approach reading instruction is to sideswipe them—to teach laterally rather than directly. To reluctant readers, learning to read must look as if it is an incidental task, as if reading is only a tool to help in learning about such things as frogs, comets or dirt bikes.

For years they have sat and plodded through books, word-by-word, and through phonics exercises, sound-by-sound. They have endured too many lessons with too little to show. When faced with the same direct instruction again, they believe it will not help this time either. Many reluctant readers quit before they begin.

To counteract their constantly verified belief of failure and in order to catch them before they quit, we must approach instruction differently. We must be willing to be led by them, using any content that will catch them; whether that be books that they can manipulate, puzzles they want to solve, personal interests, jokes, comics or any content that catches their eyes and hearts.

This sideways approach is akin to the sneaky organic cooks of the 1960s who would sneak a bit of kelp or bran into the family's food to make meals healthier without changing the taste too much or too fast. Lateral literacy instruction is based on the same idea. Let's try something different. First just a bit of "bran" or "kelp" is mixed thoroughly into something they like, then more and more as time goes by and as they accept it. Eventually the reader is no longer reluctant, maybe even eager.

Information on some specific internal and external inhibitors follows.

## Internal Self Stoppers

### Believing Says It All
Basic to everything in literacy is belief. Nothing will be accomplished without a firm belief by their teachers and parents and by the reluctant readers themselves that "they can learn to read." Too often both teachers and reluctant readers believe they will never learn. That belief in failure has to be turned into a belief in success. It is the story of *The Little*

*Engine That Could.* Even though they can, reluctant readers don't "think they can" and so don't! They must be taught to "think they can" by using a sideswiping kind of instruction.

Children's beliefs about themselves and their abilities change with the people they are around and the situations in which they find themselves. Think about the child in your classroom who last year's teacher warned you about and yet has blossomed under your care. Or the one the parent says is such a hellion at home but for you is polite and quiet. The attitudes and values you hold, and the beliefs you have toward children and teaching, are the atmosphere of your classroom and will affect the behavior of the children there. With thought, belief changes can be deliberately made. To prove this to yourself, pick out a couple of reluctant readers, watch, and then think about their behavior. Videotaping your interaction with them allows you to look at the encounters more objectively again and again. Try to identify:

- What is it you don't like?
  —maybe they always answer back in a flippant manner?
  —maybe they hide their faces and shrug?
- How do you react?
  —with sarcasm?
  —with hurt feelings and rejection?
  —by ignoring them?
- What could you do differently?
  —maybe praise their sense of the ridiculous?
  —maybe turn their answers into a word-play game?
  —maybe pair the silent ones up with talkers so they feel the safety of numbers?

Your reaction can be negative and add to their sense of failure or it can be positive and boost their belief in themselves.

### KidLink: Now, Why Did We Do That?

One way you can help your students gain control over their reading and their beliefs about reading is to introduce them to the metalevel of reading. Clue them into thinking about the "how to" of reading as they are doing it. Don't use long involved explanations, but instead, clear succinct bits now and again. Talk to them about:

- Strategies and tricks you are teaching them. Explain:
  —what they are for;
  —how to use them over and over in other reading.
- How to turn reading into a game. Use phrases such as:
  —"now, why did we do that?"

—"what if we changed...?"
—"what would happen if...?"

Clueing them into the how and why of a particular strategy gives them a useful layer of knowledge or level of awareness about reading. Changing their metalevel understanding changes their beliefs about reading automatically, without them even knowing it.

*ResearchLink:*

What a teacher believes about a reader has incredible impact. There is a famous study by Robert Rosenthal and Lonore Jacobson that proves this point. A group of teachers was told that certain children they would have in next year's class had been tested and their scores showed they would have an incredible spurt in reading growth within the coming year. Sure enough, at the end of the following year, all these children showed enormous growth in reading. The only fly in the ointment was that the children's tests were never scored and they were just randomly selected out of the whole group. The reason they leaped ahead was because their teachers had been told they would and so believed they would. Belief can move mountains!

---

*Reflection:*

Teachers and parents can change kids' beliefs about themselves and thus their reading ability by changing how they behave toward each child. Low expectations lead to failure and inadequacy. Expect reluctant kids to be able to think just as well as good readers, instruct at a higher cognitive level, exhibit confidence in their abilities and praise their successes. Treat them as if they can, believe in them, and they will.

---

## Getting Active

Reluctant readers must be engaged in reading in an active way. Most reluctant readers are either inactive or overactive, but either way their activity has nothing to do with reading. Our job is to redirect their random physical activity toward reading. Materials that beg to be touched and manipulated, strategies that require physical movement, and problem-solving puzzles and jokes all entice reluctant readers into moving. When they are moving, their minds can't help but be involved as the mind controls movement. Once their minds are involved, there is hope to catch their interest and attention.

Readers' bodies always show their mental and emotional moods and feelings through their actions. Watch your children coming into the room in the morning and from their gestures and posture, ask yourself:

- What kind of day will it be?
- Who will need my special attention?
- Who didn't get enough sleep?
- Will this need to be an active day or a quiet one?

Do these questions sound familiar? Most teachers ask these at an unconscious level. Yet we need to remind ourselves that making these questions and their answers conscious can lead to a better day. By using what you have gleaned and changing your own physical, mental and emotional reactions, you can change the atmosphere of the classroom. You can influence how your children feel and what they are willing to do as the day goes along by your own actions. If you don't regularly observe kid's behavior in this way, try choosing three children to watch for a few seconds as they come in, and see if you can predict their behavior for the day. At the closing bell, check to see how successful you were.

## KidLink: Hands On!

Reluctant readers shut down as much as possible. They are also expert at avoiding reading by being passive or acting out, and they are expert at getting the teacher to do everything. Reluctant readers have learned to perfection to get their teachers to do the reading and writing for them. We must learn to turn the tables! The best way to start is through small physical actions related to literacy. Get them physically involved by insisting they handle all materials, for example: the book, pencil, paper, game score card or any literacy material that can be manipulated.

As well as using materials that are manipulable and having reluctant kids physically handle them, use complex activities and strategies that demand physical movement such as writing, drama or walking while reading.

## ResearchLink:

As Mary Dayton-Sakari points out in her article "Struggling Readers Don't Work At Reading: They Just Get Their Teacher To!," reluctant readers behave very differently when involved with reading and writing than do good readers. Reluctant readers don't touch reading materials if they can help it, they don't hold the materials efficiently, they don't use reading materials as tools, nor do they "read with expression" or think or talk about what they are trying to read. Good readers do all of those things. They manipulate reading materials efficiently, they show the story in their faces and gestures as they "read with expression" and they discuss the content with teacher and peers. Good readers take on the task of reading and all that implies; reluctant readers avoid and leave the task to their teachers.

---

*Reflection:*

Often the best way for teachers to encourage reluctant readers to become actively involved in reading is to "stop" doing the physical work of reading for them. It is important that teachers and parents "stop":

- opening the book or holding it open;
- turning the page;
- tilting the book for their eyes;
- picking the book up off the floor;
- writing down the answers;
- taking possession of the paper and pencil.

Learn to keep your hands off. Whoever is physically involved with literacy materials becomes mentally and emotionally involved as well. That person must be the reader.

---

**Choosing to Say "Yes" or "No" to Reading**

Choice is power. In a literacy interaction, whoever picks what to read holds the power and the other person is just along for the ride. Too often it is the teacher or parent who chooses and the reluctant reader who just sits and watches. These kids have willingly given up their power over any aspect of reading and by taking over, we adults maintain their abdication. If kids have no choices, they take no risks; if they do not take risks, they are safe and their failure won't show.

It doesn't take much to give reluctant readers fairly risk-free choices. Something as simple as offering the choice between two books gives them power. Choice is not only about which book to read, it is also about what to do with the content of the book. Readers may wish to decide:

- how much of the book to read.
  - —maybe only the section on seals?
  - —maybe deciding after the first page that the book is not worth the bother?
- which bits to read and in what order.
  - —maybe just the captions?
  - —maybe starting from the back?

- what kinds of books to read.
  —maybe a magazine, a comic or a game instead of a book?
- what reading level to tackle.
  —maybe only something easy today?
  —maybe something too hard, but very interesting?
- when and where to read.
- what position to read in.
  —standing? lying? sitting?
- who to read with.
- if they'll even read today at all!

Giving choice to a kid does not mean that teachers and parents abdicate theirs. Choice for adults just becomes more hidden. It moves to a different level in that it is centered around questions such as:

- How can I introduce choice into the activity we are going to do?
- What books can I find about this topic for my reluctant readers to choose from?
- Where does instruction need to go next?
- How can I slip instruction in so the reluctant kid doesn't balk?

Choice is about allowing reluctant readers to retain ownership of and take responsibility for the specific reading process they are using and for the topics they care about. By putting choice into their hands, we allow them to feel the power and control over reading that all good readers feel.

Choices are rooted in our feelings and understandings and we constantly make them, even ones of which we are not aware. As our bodies always show our mental and emotional choices, take a moment to think about how you feel right this second. Are you: tired? anxious? calm? Name that feeling. Now smile. How does smiling make you feel? You should feel happier. The act of physically moving the muscles in your face to smile connects them via your nerves to the mind and makes you feel different. In all actions, the physical, the mental and the emotional are interconnected. When you choose whether or not to smile, you are deciding whether or not to be happy. Similarly, reluctant readers decide, when faced with reading, whether or not they want to attempt to read. If the choice is theirs, they are more likely to read.

### KidLink: The Goldilocks Sort: Too Hot, Too Cold, Just Right!

Find between 12 and 15 books whose content you think might be interesting to your reluctant readers. Just as Goldilocks chose among three bowls of porridge, ask your reluctant readers to browse through the books, then sort them into three piles that include:

- ones they would not be interested in reading;
- ones that are maybes;
- ones they would like to read.

The finished piles should give you an idea of the topics they would be willing to read about and those which they might balk over.

In a second sort you can get an idea of which genres the kids prefer by selecting books that include non-fiction, picture books, popular series, chapter books, and so on. Get your readers to sort them into piles marked:

- my kind of book;
- well, maybe;
- no thanks, not the kind of book I like.

Watch that your reluctant readers do not choose by content as in the first sort, but by genre instead. It is easier to do this sort if you choose books all on the same topic.

Want to know their reading level? For a third sort, choose books that will tell you about their independent, instructional and frustration levels. Ask the kids to sort the books into piles labeled:

- easy;
- just right;
- too hard.

It is best not to do all three sorts in one session and if, in any of these sorts, your reluctant reader comes up with only one pile—"maybes"—that tells you that they are afraid of making mistakes and need to feel safe. Try again after you have had more time together and are more comfortable with one another.

*ResearchLink:*

In a recent study by Jo Worthy, grade six reluctant readers agreed that even though they had had some positive reading experiences in school, reading was a school activity and that given the choice, they wouldn't read on their own time. They were only enthusiastic about school reading in situations where they were allowed to investigate topics of their choice and select from a wide range of books. They did not want to read what others decided they should read. In that, reluctant readers are no different than most adults. One teacher in this same study commented that she hated to read what someone else told her to read.

> *Reflection:*
> Choice isn't just about picking a book. Choice is about allowing reluctant readers to retain ownership of, and to take responsibility for, the processes in which they are engaged and the topics they care about. Putting choice into their hands allows reluctant readers to feel the power and control over reading that all good readers feel.

## Interest Leads the Way

We only really read that which catches our attention. What reluctant readers prefer to read and what teachers recommend are often quite different. They each like books for different reasons: reluctant readers want action, raw humor, familiarity and complex illustrations; teachers prefer elegance of story structure, sophistication of character development, complexity of description, irony and references to other literature. The preferences of a reluctant reader are those of a novice reader while those of a teacher are of a mature reader. We need to realize that they must crawl as readers before they can run. The topic or venue shouldn't matter, whether it is a *Hot Rod* magazine or instructions from a computer. If kids are interested, they will read it. Insistence by the teacher on any literature, whether basals, "good" stories or informational books, sets up roadblocks. A tremendous range of topics will whet reluctant readers' interest. We know everyone's interests are affected by their age, gender, reading ability, background, peers and by media in all its various forms.

When we think of finding students' interests, we automatically think of finding some subject matter, such as space, pets or turtles. Sometimes a different kind of interest will emerge: for example, the genres of fairy tales, mysteries or "Choose your Own Adventure" books. So too the structure of language itself offers an appeal in riddles, jokes, palindromes or letter writing. This leaves the question, "What else can we tap into to get reluctant readers interested enough to forget that they are learning to read and write?"

Computers? They are a real hook for some kids. Hero worship is another. Even competition, particularly competition against the self, can get kids interested enough to read. Another hook may be to get two kids interacting about some common interest. Perhaps they could create a book together. The student who feels easier with writing could do the writing, and the one who feels most comfortable with drawing could do the art work. Just think of the intellectual interaction that could go on as the writer and illustrator grope for meaning or try to understand what needs to be drawn to facilitate the writing. Look beyond the subject matter for whatever promotes the slightest spark of interest.

### KidLink: Magically, Just the Right Book

We recognize that it is not always easy to figure out what reluctant readers are truly interested in because they do not feel safe exposing any part of themselves, especially their interest in compelling topics. The key to working with these children is finding that "magic" book—the book that turns the tide and moves them beyond reluctance because they want to know. For fearful reluctant readers, the context and atmosphere of your classroom should be one meant for sharing and not shaming. Ask yourself if you:

- accept any source of reading material?
- encourage curiosity, imagination and predicting?
- foster sharing ideas?
- make reading a social event?
- eliminate "doing chores" kinds of reading?
- advocate fun reading?

Remember that the questions you ask are important but that direct questions often won't get you direct answers. Because they are hiding failure and don't want to take risks, especially with something they care about, reluctant readers are more than likely to lead you astray with their answers to a question like, "What do you like to read about?" They may say they like animals, but, in fact, not care about them at all. Keep delving. Questions like the ones below can help:

- If you could be any kind of animal, even an imaginary one, what would you be?
- If you were a super-hero, what would you do?
- If you wrote a movie or TV show, what would it be about?
- If you had a day off school, where would you go?

Beyond asking questions, be always vigilant for hints of interests dropped when reluctant readers are talking in classroom discussion and in conversation with peers, or hints in their drawings, their play or in the articles they bring to school.

### ResearchLink:

Studies by Steven Asher and the National Assessment of Educational Progress (NAEP) in Denver show that reading comprehension is related to readers' interest in the topic. In these studies, both good and poor readers performed significantly better on high-interest materials.

Readers who are interested in the topic can comprehend materials ordinarily considered to be above their reading level, as indicated by Loretta Belloni and Eugene Jongsma, as well as Jerry Johns. Joseph Vaughn notes that interest may even have more of an influence on the comprehension level of poor readers than on good ones. Any reader will try harder and put more effort into reading a topic they are interested in because there is something there they want to know. Also, they have more than the usual understanding of the topic and can predict more of the content, so they get more out of what they are reading and can be more involved in any discussion.

---

*Reflection:*

We become interested in something because we have an emotional need to know. Our interest may be in some particular information, a mind-bending puzzle or a peer interaction that engages us. Whatever hooks us, we don't see as work, even though it is. Yet clues to reluctant readers' interests are elusive, especially for the "I'll do anything you want as long as I don't have to really do anything" kind of kid. Look deeper and listen harder than normal.

---

## External Sidetrackers

### Layering the Curriculum

There is no point in worrying about whether reluctant readers receive the same curriculum as other kids. None of the other kids are really getting the exact same content anyway. Even if they are all reading from the same texts and are being exposed to the same themes, they take from the curriculum what they can and by no means all that is presented. Once reluctant readers are reading more competently, they will manage the classroom curriculum just as well as other kids. When working with reluctant readers, the important point is to get them actively involved, interested and reading something—anything!

We tend to think of curriculum as the subject matter to be taught at each grade level, but reading curriculum is not just about the subject matter. It is also about the process of learning "how to" decode and comprehend. There is, however, a third layer of curriculum that we are mostly unaware of, what Charles Galloway calls "the hidden curriculum." Backwards as it may seem, where we must start with reluctant readers is with this hidden curriculum, not with the subject matter or the process of learning how to read.

The hidden curriculum is the readers' attitudes and beliefs about themselves, their abilities and their perceptions of the value of reading and books. It is also about our attitudes and beliefs, as adults, toward the value of reading and books and toward reluctant readers and their abilities. If we believe there is something wrong with them, these kids will never show their capabilities. If we expect them to fail, they will! Edward and Evelyn Dwyer suggest that our attitudes actually influence our reluctant readers' achievements. Before they can cope with any subject matter or with the process of learning to read, we must help them turn around their negative attitudes.

To focus on addressing the hidden curriculum we need to help reluctant readers:

- develop the desire to read;
- realize they are reading, just not as well as they want to;
- believe they can learn;
- become aware of the metalevel of reading;
- understand that getting meaning, not reading each word by itself, is the point of reading;
- get over being afraid to try;
- understand that mistakes are just part of learning;
- realize that reading takes effort and practice.

The hidden curriculum is taught while teaching content and process. Attitudes, beliefs and values are always present in whatever we teach, happening in a positive or negative way whether we are aware of them or not. If we acknowledge their impact and learn to deliberately control them for the benefit of our reluctant readers, we can change their beliefs about themselves and their need to avoid reading. Then we can help them become confident readers.

## KidLink: Who Is Saying What?

To get an idea of the kinds of things you place your focus on when instructing reluctant readers, audio tape a reading interaction with one of them. Afterward, use a sheet similar to the one on the next page to tick off the different kinds of questions/comments you hear.

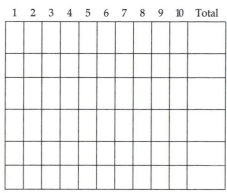

WHO IS SAYING WHAT?

Teacher questions or statements about:

| | 1 | 2 | 3 | 4 | 5 | 6 | 7 | 8 | 9 | 10 | Total |
|---|---|---|---|---|---|---|---|---|---|---|---|
| • Content | | | | | | | | | | | |
| • Reading process or skills | | | | | | | | | | | |
| • Interest or attitude | | | | | | | | | | | |
| • Controlling behavior | | | | | | | | | | | |
| • Other | | | | | | | | | | | |

Student questions or statements about:

| | 1 | 2 | 3 | 4 | 5 | 6 | 7 | 8 | 9 | 10 | Total |
|---|---|---|---|---|---|---|---|---|---|---|---|
| • Answering teacher questions | | | | | | | | | | | |
| • Content | | | | | | | | | | | |
| • Reading process or skills | | | | | | | | | | | |
| • Background knowledge | | | | | | | | | | | |
| • Attitudes or feelings | | | | | | | | | | | |
| • Other | | | | | | | | | | | |

Chances are after you have finished counting the comments in each row, you will find that you make the most comments, whether questions or statements, and that most of those comments are about behavior. Richard Anderson, as well as Jere Brophy and Thomas Good, remind us that we have long since known that teachers do more behavior control than reading instruction with reluctant readers. Usually the reluctant readers will make fewer comments than you and most of those will be answers to your questions.

### ResearchLink:

A famous study in the United States involving hundreds of classrooms reported by Russell Stauffer, and another large one in Britain by the Department of Education and Science, show that no specific reading program is distinctly better than any other, and that the teacher has more influence on reading achievement. In other words, no particular reading curriculum by itself is the best. Teachers have far more influence on pupil success than any one program.

---

*Reflection:*

There are at least three layers of curriculum in reading instruction: the content that is read; the processes and skills of decoding and comprehension; and the attitudes, beliefs and values held about reading. For reluctant readers, the hidden curriculum—how they feel about reading—must come first or the rest will never happen.

---

**Time Rules All**

Reluctant readers have perfected the art of wasting instructional and reading time; avoiding doing the work is their whole purpose. Expecting instantaneous success, they do not realize they must work at reading. If they are aware of the need to work, they are not willing to put in the time needed. Instead they waste time.

The school fosters this with a "by the bell" culture. We are driven by the bell to rush a task or come back to it tomorrow. This chunked-up system works against reluctant readers in two ways. First, like all kids, they need extended periods of time to be able to go off on tangents of interest. The "clock curriculum" doesn't allow it. Becoming engaged or finding an interest takes time. If given the time to muddle about, however, reluctant readers will become just as engaged as other kids. Second, since reluctant readers avoid reading, it takes a long time to get them started. By the time they do start, time is up and nothing has been accomplished. Day after day after day.

These kids are not dumb; they know how the system works! They know if they out-wait the teacher, they won't have to do any reading work. The answer is time—not being afraid to "waste time" and out-wait them. The use of time is part of the hidden curriculum. We must learn to teach in a different way and switch time around, becoming passive while out-waiting our reluctant readers. We must force ourselves to sit there and not do the work for them. Once kids understand that the reading is up to them, they begin to work, to become involved and to make choices. Ultimately, if we won't do the work, they have to.

Because of our constant awareness of passing time, this approach may not seem productive. Yet it is. In the beginning, out-waiting reluctant readers seems to take forever, but over the long haul they give in, do the work, get faster at it, and, finally, the teacher doesn't need to worry about time on task again.

How much "wait time" do you actually allow yourself with reluctant readers? Go back to the audio tape you created in the last section. For each time you ask a question or make a comment that requires the reluctant reader to answer, count off the seconds between when you finish asking and either the reluctant reader answers or you answer your own question, make a comment or ask another question.

You can do a mathematical average if you want, but, even without it, it is fairly easy to see the trend of how much wait time you allow. It would also be interesting to compare, via audio tape count, the wait time you allow for a reluctant reader versus what you allow for a good reader or during a discussion with the whole class.

⊚ *ResearchLink:*
Jean Guthrie reminds us, that as simple and commonsensical as it seems, we must become more aware of this fact: kids get better at reading in direct proportion to the amount of time they spend reading books that are easy enough for them. Richard Anderson points out that we also know that the more time given over to reading in the classroom, the bigger the yearly gains on standardized tests. To get better at reading it must be practiced a lot, and practiced by really reading, not doing worksheets.

---

*Reflection:*
School "time" works both against and for reluctant readers. There is never time for sustaining engagement when kids must constantly move from one subject to another. School time also works for reluctant readers in a sort of perverse way because since we are always in a hurry, if they wait long enough, we teachers will do the work.

---

### In Our Image

As teachers and parents in today's world, we have more than enough excuses for neglecting the literacy modeling our children need from us. As parents, we may not be able to be there when our children come home from school. We may also be raising our children on our own, while running the house as a second or third job. The stresses and strains of daily life do not lend themselves to our being perfect parents or teachers. What happens though, is that because of our constant stress, our kids do not get the positive modeling of literacy activities, nor the help they may need along the way.

After an unending day of work, sitting down and reading to our children often seems like the last thing we have the strength to do, but in fact, if done in a positive, humorous way, reading and talking with our children can relieve our stress and calm our nerves. Daily reading in the classroom can also calm nerves and help build better relationships.

Another factor that hinders many adults from being good reading models for children is that they have become "self-designated non-readers." Adult self-designated non-readers don't read much more than the stop sign and the television guide, but they often don't even realize they don't read. These individuals:

- do not talk about books;
- never go to the library;
- are too busy to read;
- have no visible personal reading program in evidence;
- may be television couch potatoes.

It is impossible for a non-reading teacher or parent to instill a love of books and reading in children. If we want reluctant kids to become readers, somehow the time and inclination must be found. After all, teachers are paid to read!

### KidLink: Mirror, Mirror on the Wall

What kind of a reading model are you in the classroom? the home? Do you portray a good reader or a reluctant reader? To help you find out, ask yourself the questions shown below and on the next page.

---

*AS A TEACHER, WHAT KIND OF A READING MODEL ARE YOU?*

- Do you read aloud to your class?
  —Everyday?
  —From information materials, as well as fiction?
- Do you do sustained silent reading in your classroom?
  —Do you read a book during SSR?
  —Do you share the good parts?
  —Do you ever read non-fiction?
- Do you regularly read children's literature?
  —Can you talk about current "cool" books?
  —Do you buy books for your classroom?

---

- Do you read for interest and fun?
- Do you read to your children every day?
- Do you tell them stories?
- Do you encourage questions and comments from them during your reading?
- Do you share your ideas or only tell your children what to do next?
- Do you answer their questions?
- Do you probe their ideas and inferences by asking "why" questions?
- Do you deliberately try to enrich their ideas and expand their vocabulary by visiting places of interest and by taking trips?

In other words, in all these ways, do you engage their minds and encourage deeper thinking?

If you answered "no" to most of the above questions, you may wish to try some of these strategies to become a better reading role model:

- Find favorite authors.
- Read what you like to read; for example, information books, hobby-related titles, cookbooks, etc.
- Talk to friends about good books.
- Borrow (or steal) books from friends.
- Use the best seller lists to find books of interest.
- Link to Oprah Winfrey's or other book club's suggestions.
- Try that novel you see on television.
- Read any book that catches your interest.
- Go out of your way to make time to read.
- Read yourself to sleep.
- Have a book at hand for when you have to wait.
- Question what you are reading as you read to your class or child to help them develop story and informational schema, build concepts and develop their vocabulary, as suggested by Jim Trelease in *The New Read-Aloud Handbook.*

⑨ *ResearchLink:*

That parents are their kids first teachers is "common wisdom" and has been supported by several research studies. Karen Thomas concludes that the social interactions between parents and children, the clarification of concepts and the systematic approach to print practiced by many parents are examples of good teaching practice. In another study by Elfrieda Hiebert, three parent behaviors were found to be highly related to reading acquisition: engaging children in informal, game-like activities; directing attention to the relationships between spoken and written words; and feeling responsible for teaching literacy skills.

---

*Reflection:*

As well as modeling for our kids, adult self-designated non-readers must become deliberately aware of why they are not reading, of the times and places in their schedule that would work for reading and of the kinds of books they would really enjoy reading. If you don't like fiction, don't read it; read information books, magazines, from the Web or ....

---

## Reluctant Readers Must Take Charge

As Marie Clay says, reluctant readers will never read until they feel inner control over the act of reading. As reading teachers, our real job is to help reluctant readers gain that control. In her study, Mary Dayton-Sakari shows that readers' inner control or lack of it is reflected in their outer control. To allow inner control to manifest itself, we must insist reluctant readers take on outer control of the materials, content and interaction between themselves and their teachers.

Helping reluctant readers gain outer control means we must pay attention to the smallest, seemingly most insignificant details—those things we always take for granted and just accept as the way things are. Sometimes seeing, then acting on one little, easily-dismissed detail can make such a big difference. The thing to always be watchful for is "What is this child not doing that makes it hard for him to succeed?" and then not to ignore or dismiss what we see as unimportant.

We have to offer every opportunity for kids to take charge and make reading decisions, no matter how insignificant; often, the smaller the step the better. The reader must be made to choose the pencil, the paper, the book, the game score card, even the place to sit. Every move in the reading interaction must become open for option and choice. Some of these opportunities are easy to see but others are as subtle as who takes the book out of the book bag or who picks the pencil up off the floor. This kind of observation requires moment-by-moment consciousness. The more we become aware of control and refuse to take charge the better. Once reluctant readers accept the responsibility of control over reading, it becomes a habit, a way of operating. Reading, then, becomes not foreign or impossible any more, but attainable.

Despite the need to put as much control as possible into the hands of reluctant readers, there are aspects of instruction that really belong to teachers and should remain within our control. The materials, procedure, content and place to read are legitimate choices for them and we should stay out of their way as much as possible. But the overview of where the child is developmentally and the goals that govern where we have gone and still need to go should be in our hands.

Internal decisions such as "Is this sidetrack we seem to be on getting us anywhere?" must be ours. The sneaked-in questions, discussion and activities that prod development are also ours. The searching and supplying of materials reluctant readers may not think of or have access to are ours. All these choices belong to us. Yet, we must keep in mind that at some point reluctant readers will take complete control and become their own teachers. Also, we must always keep in mind that the long way round, allowing readers to choose their own way, may in fact get us where we want to go faster than our seemingly more direct way.

⊚ *KidLink: Who Is in Charge?*

How much do you control the literacy materials as compared to your reluctant readers? Videotape yourself during a reading interaction with a reluctant reader. Later, while viewing the video, tick off every time you touch any literacy materials used in the interaction, such as the book, paper or pencil. Now count how many times the reluctant reader touches them. If you are like other teachers, Mary Dayton-Sakari suggests that you will touch the materials just as much or more than reluctant readers. You are in control. You might also try taping yourself with a good reader and make a similar count. Again, if you are like most teachers, you will not bother to touch the materials much at all. The good reader, not you, is in control.

⊚ *ResearchLink:*

Results from several studies on children taking control over their school learning suggest that they can take on self-management and academic responsibilities and that their beliefs in their ownership of control affect their reactions to outside expectations. Indeed, it has been shown by Margaret Wang that as they exert control, their performance improves. What we do in the classroom to allow kids to take control or not makes a difference in whether they do or not.

*Reflection:*
Reluctant readers will not become confident readers until they take charge of their own learning. We only hinder their progress by doing the reading work for them. Start with small steps of letting go. Become the passive partner, then take less and less responsibility for the actual act of reading.

# 4 ∗ User-Friendly Entry Points for Reluctant Readers

*A good book is a good book is a good book!*

There is more than one way into reading, more than one kind of material to read and a host of different formats from which to choose. As teachers and librarians we often clutch onto favorite titles that we know will be successful. With reluctant readers we need to focus, not on the books we like, but on the ones they like. To extend what they know about, we need to remind ourselves that it is up to us to be aware of the possibilities of resources for their interests. We have to be able to "see" the potential appeal of the hosts of formats, topics and titles which kids are currently reading, not all of which we put into our school libraries.

We, as teachers, are responsible for giving students the freedom to explore a whole range of reading materials, selecting tidbits here and there to satisfy their curiosity and interests. Many primary-looking resources are indeed most suitable because of their reading level and appropriateness, yet kids need reassurance and permission that it is alright to read these easy books. We need to provide the security to read short sections of books and to browse freely and openly throughout any section of a title. Teacher modeling as a regular classroom practice is important. Believe it or not, even adults do not have to read a book thoroughly from cover to cover!

In this chapter, we shall include many categories of reading resources that, at varying times, will appeal to reluctant readers. We have to rely on their choice of interests and move with them as they quickly change from one interest to the next. There are books that will instantly attract them, such as the photographic appeal of the many information books produced by Dorling Kindersley in the *Eyewitness* series.

Teachers and parents should be reminded that teacher librarians, public librarians and knowledgeable bookstore staff are excellent resources for specific titles that will entice reluctant readers. Most public libraries have lists of books devised for just this purpose, as do we in the final bibliography of this book.

## Move It! Books with Physical Interactive Movement

> Physical- - - - - - - - - - - - - - Movement - - - - - - - - - - - - - Manipulation

Reluctant readers need books that force actual touching and physical manipulation. Whether it is by flipping a flap, turning the book around or even upside down, kids become inadvertently involved in the process of reading. This is reminiscent of the first stage of becoming a reader where pre-readers love "mucking" about with books that invite manipulation.

The physical nature of interacting with books, particularly those that have something to feel, move or control in some way, redirects reluctant readers' attention by connecting their physical behavior to their thinking. An opportunity to manipulate some aspect of a book helps channel the hectic energy of overactive kids. Passive, underactive kids are also forced to engage because, as they physically handle a book, they get mentally involved. Any movement that gets their mental gears in motion, gets them thinking. Therefore, if that movement is connected to reading, the thinking will be too.

### Hands On

The following titles are particularly well suited for getting reluctant readers physically involved. We have placed examples of pop-ups and how-to titles in separate sections.

Brown, Ruth. *If At First You Do Not See.* Depicts the scary adventures of a caterpillar. Readers must turn the book around to read the text along the sides of the pages. As it is turned over, a new illustration is revealed.
Carle, Eric. *Hello, Red Fox.* Although designed as a means for younger children to explore primary colors, it is fascinating to all. Just stare at the dot within

the red heart (or object) for ten seconds and then see what happens when you stare at a dot on a white page. Prepare to be surprised. It works!

Cassidy, John. *Earthsearch: A Kid's Geography Museum in a Book.* An instant "touch me and get involved" approach is used with great visuals, super flaps, moveables and even coins. Another title is *Explorabook: A Kid's Science Museum in a Book.*

Delafosse, Claude. *Animals* (A First Discovery Art Book*).* Overlapping acetate sheets intrigue readers to look again at famous art works. Other titles in the series include: *Portraits, Landscapes* and *Paintings.*

Dicks, Ian and David Hawcock. *Unwrap the Mummy! A Four-foot-long, Fact-filled, Pop-up Mummy to Explore!* This almost life-sized, folded flap-book delves into the inner and outer parts of an Egyptian mummy. It includes related information on pyramid building and mummification.

Harris, Nicholas. *Into the Rain Forest* (The Nature Company EcoXplorer Series). Each page in this book is cut into three flaps to allow different scenes of the rain forest.

Hawcock, David. *The Amazing Pop-up, Pull-out Space Shuttle.* Filled with space facts, this package unfolds to reveal a 1.2-metre-high model for hanging on the wall.

Ling, Mary. *Wild Animal Go-Round: Turn the Wheel and See the Animals Grow.* Animals such as penguins, zebras, giraffes, corn snakes, ostriches, tigers and elephants are seen from birth to adulthood via photos on a moveable wheel. See also *Animal Go-Round.*

Martin, Terry. *Open House: A Lift-the-flap Book.* Features include a Roman street, Scottish tower (watch out for the man sitting on the edge of the outhouse!), Dutch home and Japanese house. Has over 90 flaps.

Moscovich, Ivan. *The Think Tank.* An engrossing collection of 25 pop-up and 3D games and puzzles. The clever folding of a double image jigsaw puzzle reveals Marilyn Monroe on one side and the Mona Lisa on the other.

Nilsen, Anna. *Terrormazia: A Hole New Kind of Maze Game.* An interactive, multidimensional maze book for those who seek adventure.

*Our Changing Planet* (Voyages of Discovery). Features a dramatic geologic view of the earth with shiny black backgrounds, surprising split pages, acetate overlays and a raised surface of the earth's crust. There are 18 titles in this series.

Pelham, David. *Sam's Pizza!* Explore your own multi-layered small pizza. Each layer contains surprises under the flaps. A delicious experience.

Pelham, David. *The Sensational Samburger.* Presented as a "delicious," 3-D, multi-layered, paper-engineered, mock hamburger. Two kids make a pretend, bug-infested sandwich for their burger-stealing dog. He eats it. Gross!

*Puzzle Gallery: Pets.* This book includes five jigsaw puzzles, each framed within a page and featuring pets in famous paintings. Kids are directed to note unusual details.

*Space Shuttle and Hubble Telescope: Cross-Section Puzzle.* A jigsaw puzzle with 200 pieces requires kids to recognize the mechanical components of the space shuttle while they read about each type.

Tolhurst, Marilyn. *Knights: The Age of Adventure to Unlock and Discover.* Contained in a treasure chest, this kit includes a book, game and an assemble-your-own castle, map and medieval catapult. Others in the series include *Aztecs, Egyptians* and *Vikings.*

*Under the Sea.* One of the Discovery Box series which includes a book and an activity kit. This one, looking at life in the ocean depths, is highlighted with see-through, dark, acetate sheets. When readers build the model sub, they are able to explore underwater with a pretend beam of light. Other titles include *Time, Stencils* and *Prehistoric Life.*

### ⑨ *ComputerLink: Play It Again*

Computer programs can offer as much movement and manipulation as interactive books do, as long as they truly involve the kids. The importance of computers in this instance is in the actual physical movement of the kids' hands on the keyboard and the mouse. Through this physical activity they become engaged in the process and ultimately in the content. Yes, there can be value in the games that kids play over and over on the computer, as long as they gradually get weaned away to become more involved with more text.

---

*Reflection:*
When kids are actively engaged with interactive books or computer games they are not worried about having to read them. Be aware that moving physically gets us involved mentally.

---

### Pop-ups

Pop-up and flap books fascinate people of all ages, primarily due to the great appeal of their moving parts. We all love to pull the tabs or flip the flaps to make things happen. We've got "power!" Quality titles often include a large amount of information, and even if it is squeezed into small print, kids don't seem to mind—only adults do! While these books do not have a long life span, it is worth the cost to see reluctant readers showing these books to others who have not seen them before. It is wonderful to see them sharing the thrill and pleasure of success in predicting and knowing what is going to happen.

One of the most complicated pop-up books is Jonathan Miller's *The Human Body,* designed by David Pelham with its detailed views of the workings of the inner parts of the body. It is interesting to note that it took over 45 minutes to assemble this book after the pages were printed. Here are some others to explore:

Allen, Jonathan. *Wake Up, Sleeping Beauty! An Interactive Book With Sounds*. A prince and his assistant try to wake up a princess, but despite gongs and symbols that make a lot of noise, it just doesn't work. As they leave, the young boy says goodbye with a kiss and she wakes up. The power of a kiss!

*Dinosaur Hunt: A Pull-out, Pop-up Discovery*. This thin book is a surprise. Open it by sections and out folds a 3-D Tyrannosaurus Rex skeleton to hang on the wall.

Fornari, Giuliano. *Inside the Body: A Lift-the-flap Book*. Double-sized spreads reveal a human body; open the flaps to reveal muscle, blood, food and breathing functions, as well as the skeleton.

Harris, Peter. *Have You Seen Max!* A rascal cat keeps hiding in a haunted house.

Howe, James. *Bunnicula Escapes! A Pop-up Adventure*. A family's pet rabbit escapes at a county fair, with hair-raising experiences.

Pelham, David. *Say Cheese!* Shaped like a wedge of cheese, this book is complete with mock mouseholes. In it, Grandma mouse decides it's time to have a family get-together. Hold still for the photo. Cheese!

Sabuda, Robert. *ABC Disney: An Alphabet Pop-up*. Hidden behind fingerpainted panels, Disney characters dramatically pop out at the reader; Hercules flexes his muscles, Kao the python slithers forward, the Queen bellows forth and the White Rabbit scurries off!

Taylor, David. *Nature's Creatures of the Dark: A Pop-up, Glow-in-the-Dark Exploration*. Open the book and out pops a bat, glowworm, owl and giant squid. Each is cunningly surrounded by photos, illustrations and lots of facts.

van der Meer, Ron and Dr. Alan McGowan. *Sailing Ships*. This is one of the most awesome pop-up productions because of the magical effect of three-dimensional models rising from the pages of the book.

Whitman, John. *Star Wars: The Death Star*. Come inside the … "secret chambers of the Empire's most devastating weapon as it hurtles through space on its mission of destruction."

Woelfein, Luise. *Forest Animals*. A series of clues are provided for an octet of animals in various countries. Open the flaps and the animals pop out. Another title in this series is *Desert Animals*.

Wood, Audrey. *The Napping House Wakes Up*. Enjoy this hilarious moveable edition of a favorite cumulative tale.

Young, Jay. *The Most Amazing Science Pop-up Book*. Packed with information and devices, the book includes a pop-up microscope, a camera obscura, a kaleidoscope and a periscope.

## KidLink: Make Your Own Pop-up

The value in kids making their own pop-ups is that they are required to do some reading and writing but only in small amounts: in words, phrases or short sentences. With the focus on creating the illustrations, working with text does not seem so overwhelming. A super resource is Joan Irvine's *How to Make Pop-ups!*

## How To

The use of a book to learn "how to" do something provides another level of interacting with the text. Instead of manipulating the actual pages, kids use the book as a prop to help them in creating something. There are books that show how to make puppets, models, paper airplanes, knots, cootie catchers, origami and much more.

Cookbooks for kids are currently best sellers. See the KidLink "Bake Me!" at the end of this section for a number of cookbooks for kids. Many interesting how-to titles have been created by the Klutz company, a firm filling a unique niche in the educational market. Their creative output has benefited many reluctant readers.

Especially clear and easy-to-follow directions are offered in the following books:

Cassidy, John and Michael Stroud. *The Klutz Book of Magic.* "When was the last time you were truly astounding?" 31 tricks and 5 props do just that.

Cassidy, John. *The Klutz Book of Knots.* A board book complete with cord, helpful holes, illustrations and directions for 24 knots including a magic one to tie.

Cole, Joanna and Stephanie Calmenson. *Marbles: 101 Ways to Play.* In addition to explaining how to shoot a marble, lagg, and talk about bombsies, friendlies, fudging, fulking, keepsies and knuckle down, the authors offer clear instructions on a bevy of circle, hole and shooting games.

*The Cootie Catcher Book.* Reveals the secrets of making folded paper fortune tellers with eight made and twelve make-your-own versions.

Gryski, Camilla. *Camilla Gryski's Favourite String Games.* Sixteen figures with clear illustrations for how to hold your hands and the strings for different string games. Pieces of colored string are included too!

## KidLink: Bake Me!

All kids, especially boys, love to eat!

Feeding yourself is a basic survival skill, so encouraging reluctant readers to cook makes a lot of sense. The children's publishing scene, similar to that for adults, is providing more cookbooks every year. Often for kids, these may well relate to literary favorites such as *Little House on the Prairie, Anne of Green Gables* and *Mother Goose.*

Encourage the kids to read recipes, then make two lists: one for what they have and one for what they need. This is good for reluctant readers because they can look at the page and copy it. It is practice, but not a pain. Following this, they can actually go with an adult to buy the necessary ingredients and return to make the treat. Reading labels and instructions to make the treat provides good incidental reading practice. Sharing the delicious results gives kids an awesome feeling of success and status. This strategy is not meant to be an edible disaster! A few "tasty" cookbooks for kids include:

Fison, Josie and Felicity, Dahl. *Roald Dahl's Revolting Recipes.* Related to Dahl's books, the cleverly amusing illustrations that accompany the recipes feature Josie Fison's photos of real food inserted within the sketches.
*KidsCooking: A Very Slightly Messy Manual.* This spiral-bound, deftly-organized cookbook also includes nonedibles such as play dough, face paint and dog biscuits.
Linton, Marilyn. *Just Desserts and Other Treats for Kids to Make.* A delicious reading experience featuring numbered steps to follow.
Pulleyn, Micah and Sarah Bracken. *Kids in the Kitchen: 100 Delicious, Fun and Healthy Recipes to Cook and Bake.* It makes you hungry just to look at the photographs of the food!
Wilder, Laura Ingalls (with recipes by Amy Cotler). *My Little House Cookbook.* Includes eleven, simple recipes ranging from breakfast sausage balls, to creamy oatmeal, lemonade, butter cookies and strawberry jam; all related to the Little House books.
Wilkes, Angela. *The Children's Step-by-Step Book.* A visual feast of scrumptuous eggs, salads, pastas, meats, breads and desserts.
Winston, Mary, ed. *American Heart Association Kids' Cookbook.* Recipes are presented with clear illustrations, appropriate lists and numbered steps. Snacks, soups, entrees and beverages are included.

## Gotcha! Books with Mental Involvement and Problem Solving

Mental Involvement - - - Problem Solving - - - Puzzles, Games, Humor

The challenge we all face is in getting kids to think actively at a deeper level. Reluctant readers just don't think for themselves. They follow directions, do what they are told to do and never question. The point of getting them mentally involved is to get them to do some thinking for themselves and to become more creative in their thinking, rather than following what someone else tells them to do. It should be remembered that when we are physically active, we are also more mentally active and alert.

Puzzles, games and jokes, which are sometimes physical, also require mental activity. Reluctant readers love figuring out the answer ahead of others, and, as they already know the solution, they gain the sheer pleasure of sharing the book with someone who doesn't know. In this way, they experience the power of knowledge and of thinking for themselves. Their intelligence can shine—an occurrence that is rare when they read. Grappling with a puzzle is so much better than grappling with vocabulary. Metacognitively, it actually forces them to engage, creating a desire to read.

## Puzzlers

The following are some titles that require kids to quest after solutions. Have fun with the following:

### Games

Cole, Joanna and Stephanie Calmenson. *Crazy Eights and Other Card Games.* Easy-to-read illustrated instructions for over twenty games plus information on how to handle the cards.

Drake, Jane and Ann Love. *The Kids Cottage Games Book.* Great for a vacation—a bevy of indoor, outdoor and water games. Some just for one or two players, and even games to make.

Harper, Piers. *Snakes and Ladders and Hundreds of Mice!* Can you make a plan to rescue a silly cat who has climbed to the top of Tottering Tower?

Hoban, Tana. *Just Look.* A circular hole allows the reader to guess what the circular inch reveals: a penguin, giraffe, tower or rabbit?

Miller, Marvin. *Codemaster: Book 1.* How to write and decode secret messages including a cardboard, pull-out, decoder wheel. Also consult Book 2.

*Puzzles and Puzzlers.* Optical illustrations, word searches and animals to guess by their eyes and tracks are just a peek into this pocket-size, animal-orientated book.

*Scrabble Puzzles.* Over 100 unfinished challenges. Easy and expert solutions and target scores.

Townsend, Charles. *World's Most Perplexing Puzzles.* Full of one-page "thinking" puzzles from the world's most perplexing "match" puzzle to the world's most perplexing "lunch tray" puzzle. Answers in back. Many other titles in the series.

### Riddles and Jokes

Hall, Katy and Lisa Eisenberg. *Fishy Riddles.* Cast your line to get hooked by these hilariously witty riddles.

McMullan, Kate. *The Frog Prince Drinks Diet Croak and Other Wacky Fairy Tale Jokes.* Full of ridiculous riddles based on children's background knowledge of fairy tales and nursery rhymes.

Walton, Rick and Ann. *I Toad You So: Riddles About Frogs and Toads.* Lots of groans and croaks will result when the riddles are asked.

### Story Games

Anderson, Scoular. *A Puzzling Day in the Land of the Pharoahs: A Search-and-Solve Gamebook.* When a class's field trip to a museum results in their being zapped back to Egyptian times, students try to find hidden objects in the detailed illustrations.

Burston, Patrick. *The Planet of Terror* (A Choose Your Challenge Gamebook). How to find a lost spaceship on the Planet of Terror and blast back to Earth!

Cushman, Doug. *The Mystery of King Karfu*. The greatest detective, Seymour Sleuth, is off to Egypt to solve the case of the missing stone chicken, and he shares his notes on the case. A secret code solves the real mystery.

Dixon, Andy. *Sword Quest* (An Usborne Fantasy Adventure). Seeking to retrieve a stolen sword, readers are invited to join three knights as they enter the Castle of Glee in the ancient Kingdom of Gladlands. Absolutely filled with details, readers must find clues as they view the zany action.

Golden, Christopher. *The 10-Minute Detective: 25 Scene-of-the-Crime Mystery Puzzles You Can Solve Yourself*. Detective Justin Case teases our thinking ability.

Jonas, Ann. *The 13th Clue*. Page after page of picture word clues leading down a path to a surprise ending.

Neuman, Marjorie. *Hornpipe's Hunt for Pirate Gold: A Puzzle Storybook*. Younger readers delight in finding specific details in the illustrations.

O'Brien, Eileen and Diana Riddell. *The Usborne Book of Secret Codes*. Reveals confidential communication styles ranging from letter swap, to Morse, to calendar, to snail and newspaper. Invisible writing too!

## ComputerLink: Risk It!

Computer-based involvement is very important for reluctant readers. Its appeal is that it is fast-paced, immediate, can be done individually or shared with a friend, and requires making sense out of puzzling statements. With computers, kids are willing to take risks they won't take with books. The risk just does not seem to be as threatening, probably because there is no danger in guessing. Guessing is one of many mental strategies that kids can call on at will. Scientists use guessing as an inquiry strategy all the time. The goal is not to have one right answer but the stretching of thinking and thought-devising possibilities for these kids.

Web sites or CD-ROMs offer innumerable possibilities for problem solving and thought stretching on the part of reluctant readers. Check out the Magic School Web site for further details about this series at *http//scholastic.com/MagicSchoolBus*. These CD-ROMs are worth a look too:

*The Magic School Bus Explores the Solar System: A Fun-filled, Fact-packed Science Adventure!* The kids are put in the driver's seat as they try to find the teacher Mrs. Frizzle's hiding place.

*I Spy: Brain-Building Games for Kids!* "Over 1300 object-and-word searches built into hundreds of riddles, puzzles and activities!"

## KidLink: Give Me a Clue

Ask the kids, working in pairs or trios, to write out five to eight clues describing an object. Have them write these on paper slips and place them in a paper bag for secret withdrawing. Another group of kids then draws out one clue at a time until they can guess the object.

Are you ready? Your clues are the following:

- transparent;
- bubbling;
- refreshing;
- hard on the outside and hard/soft on the inside;
- without the outside it will escape;
- sharp tasting;
- cold at first and then warmer;
- pale buttercup color.

Did you clue in? It's a refreshing glass of lemonade—or champagne if you are so inclined!

## KidLink: AWOL Game

Similar to the "give me a clue" strategy above, our "away without leave" game uses a more-than-one-meaning word to be guessed. Three or four sentences, which contain the chosen word, are created as clues. The acronym "AWOL" is substituted for the word in each sentence. For example:

- He won't AWOL the ball.
- I AWOL my cat.
- AWOL Smith is our new teacher.
- Sean will have to AWOL going to the movie; he is sick.

What is the AWOL word? "Miss" of course!

### Search and Find

The *Waldo* series is another great phenomenon for all ages. It has proven to be a highly successful series in many countries, giving an opportunity for readers to be instantly involved in the search for Waldo. To assure the continued success of Martin Handford's *Where's Waldo?*, revised editions have been done featuring a bevy of intriguing characters that accompany him. Some *Waldo* titles include: *Where's Waldo? 2nd Ed.; Where's Waldo? The Fantastic Journey; Where's Waldo? In Hollywood; Where's Waldo Now? 2nd Ed.*

"Now with eye-boggling extras!," the reader literally needs to get into the books to find all of them. There is the possibility for a lot of talk about who is in the detailed illustrations, accompanied by much good humor and clever wit. Check it out on the web at *www.FindWaldo.com*.

Very sophisticated forerunners of the *Waldo* books are those by Mitsumasa Anno. Hundreds of historical and literary characters and places are cleverly included in such titles as *Anno's Journey, Anno's Brit-*

*ain* and *Anno's Aesop: A Book of Fables* by Aesop and Mr. Fox. Other search-and-find books include:

Alles, Hemesh, illus., with S.A.J. Wood. *Errata: A Book of Historical Errors.* Can you find ten errors in each of twelve scenes from past civilizations? Did you miss the knight riding the bike in the Bayeux tapestry?

Heywood, Rosie. *The Great City Search.* Includes eleven elaborately detailed sites in the city, each offering a challenge to the reader to locate a myriad seagulls, types of boats, helicopters, buses, as well as ten specific individuals.

Khanduri, Kamini. *The Great World Tour.* Eighteen places in the world are portrayed in unique, highly detailed illustrations. In each, readers are challenged to find eighteen people and animals, as well as cultural items of each country. You really have to look!

Marzolla, Jean. *I Spy Super Challenger: A Book of Picture Riddles.* Startling views of a mess of objects you have to find after reading the riddles. See also *I Spy Mystery, I Spy Spooky Night* and other titles.

Rogers, Paul. *What Can You See?* A child, a dirigible balloon and a telescope: features things to see from the air as she travels across the city, county and along the sea.

Steiner, Joan. *Look-Alikes: Discover a Land Where Things Are Not As They Appear.* Incredible vistas created entirely of ordinary objects to give vast 3-D perspectives. Try to find the glove sofa, sweater building, scissor Ferris wheel and coffee pot engine. Amazingly, the more you look, the more you see!

Tallarico, Tony. *What's Wrong Here? At School.* A dozen or more things are wrong on each double-page spread.

---

*Reflection:*

For reluctant readers, grappling with solutions to puzzles, figuring out a joke or riddle, or posing problems doesn't seem like reading since it requires an intense mental effort. But it is reading—after all, what is reading but understanding and comprehending?

---

## Know What? Books with Engaging Information

Desires - - - - - - - - - - - - - - - Interest - - - - - - - - - - Information/Facts

If there is an area of children's literature that has improved dramatically and exploded in number in the last few years it is that of information books. A major factor has been the introduction of the "Eyewitness books" from England by Dorling Kindersley. This remarkable company now has hundreds of titles available, often co-published in many countries. They specialize in bright white pages, glossy photographs of many sizes, short snappy print sections and lots of facts. A splendid example is *The Dorling Kindersley Visual Encyclopedia*, which they say has over 50,000 essential facts, figures and dates. In its 456 pages, it covers a wealth of information and is perfect for visual browsing. Eye-catching labeled illustrations, a seamless flow of facts and useful charts often catch the reader's interest and timelines capture the attention of readers with a particular interest in the topic.

Many reluctant readers are not story kids—they are, in fact, information kids. They want to know how things work and why things are the way they are. "Interest" in the world around them is the key component. Therefore, it goes without saying that teachers have to constantly keep alert for visible signs of what these kids are interested in now. This could well be influenced by their television viewing habits, but also by their peer group, current movies and by the latest fashions and fads. We can connect to many reluctant readers through their information interests because this is where their feelings are, where their concerns are and where their desire to know lies. Studies show that kids will read two levels above their usual reading level if they want to know about a topic.

## Information Books

### Topical Books

Books that might command kids' interest abound in the bookstores and comprise an impressive range of topics. Not all topics are covered in our selection but some that we recommend include:

Ainsworth, Ken. *Building a Solitaire Game and a Peg Board* (Building Together Series). A dad helps his daughter to safely build a game board. See also: *Building a Shelf and a Bike Rack*.

Arnold, Caroline. *Monkey*. Photo essay on the daily life of a red-crowned mangabey in its zoo home. Other titles include: *Kangaroo, Zebra, Giraffe* and *Cheetah*.

Ash, Russell. *Incredible Comparison*. Large-format, cross-sectional comparisons of mountains, disasters, items great and small or light and heavy, into space, into the solar system, buildings, speed and capacity. Incredible details in illustrations and text snippets.

Baker, Lucy. *Life in the Deserts: Animals, People, Plants*. What has humans' influence been on this fragile environment? Many photos. Other titles include: *Oceans, Rainforests* and *Polar Lands*.

Biesty, Stephen. *Castle* (Stephen Biesty's Cross-Sections). An incredibly detailed examination of all aspects of the construction of a castle.

Dewin, Ted, illus., with Steve Parker. *Inside the Whale and Other Animals.* Awesome x-ray illustrations showing the inside structure of animals.

Goodall, Jane. *The Chimpanzee Family Book.* Photographic essay on the life of a special family group.

Gryski, Camilla. *Hands On, Thumbs Up, Secret Handshakes, Fingerprints, Sign Languages and More Handy Ways to Have Fun with Hands.* How do our hands work, how can we talk with them and how can we use them in play?

Hockman, Hilary, ed. *What's Inside? Everyday Things.* Simple views of the insides of such things as a washer, iron, camera and clock.

Kent, Peter. *Hidden Under the Ground: The World Beneath Your Feet.* Cutaway views of such subterranean places as tombs, dungeons, mines and animal burrows.

Kindersley, Barnabas and Anabel. *Celebrations!* (Children Just Like Me). A variety of children are pictured celebrating in festivals and special days in many countries.

Langley, Andrew and Philip de Souza. *The Roman News: The News!* Read all about it! A glimpse of Roman history, culture and daily life in newspaper form.

Ling, Mary and Mary Atkinson. *The Snake Book.* A dozen boas, vipers, constrictors and pythons—snakes to view close-up in safety. Amazing photography.

Maynard, Christopher. *Informania: Sharks.* Coil-bound format with great visuals of sharks to intrigue the reader.

Orr, Richard. *Nature Cross-Sections.* Large-format views of inner details of natural formations including a beaver lodge, termite city, rain forest, beehive, oak tree, arctic terrain and the desert.

Steele, Philip. *Step Into the Roman Empire.* The Roman world comes alive with how-to instructions for making models of a temple, armor, amphora, headdress and other objects.

Stott, Carole. *Night Sky* (Eyewitness Explorers). A small handbook of the moon, stars and planets.

Swanson, Diane. *A Toothy Tongue and One Long Foot: Nature Activities for Kids.* A collection of seasonal projects including predicting rain, inspecting insects and sizing a tree.

Tuyen, Pham Dinh. *Classic Origami.* Seventy-nine pages of basic to complex forms of this Japanese paper folding art. Simple directions with clear photographs.

Watts, Barrie, illus. *See How They Grow: Mouse.* Mice grow fast—see it for yourself!

Wilcox. Charlotte. *Mummies and Their Mysteries.* How many cultures have the custom of mummification to preserve their dead?

Wood, Jenny. *Jungles: Facts, Stories, Activities.* Close-up photos and illustrations depict life in the tropical regions. Another title is *Caves.*

## Number or Counting Books

One school subject that many reluctant readers are rather good at is mathematics. Their minds work well with numbers and they are intrigued by finding math solutions. Books about math concepts, while they do have reading in them, give these kids a better chance at success because they have the math background knowledge to help figure out unknown words. Here are a few they might enjoy:

Anno, Mitsumasa. *Anno's Counting Book.* Prepare to be challenged by numbers and images.

Brooks, Alan. *Frogs Jump: A Counting Book.* A hilarious 1 to 12 book, with delightful Kelloggian animals wearing tank tops sporting their numbers.

Johnson, Stephen T. *City by Numbers.* Quick, can you spot the number in the city scene?

McGrath, Barbara. *The M & M's Counting Book.* An easy-to-read math counting book; sets, addition and subtraction with yummy chocolate candies.

Micklethwait, Lucy. *I Spy Two Eyes: Numbers in Art.* Twenty famous works of art, each containing the equivalent number of objects, for example, Lucas Cranach the Elder's "Madonna and Child Under An Apple Tree" has sixteen apples.

Murphy, Stuart. *A Pair of Socks* (Mathstart). Matching, a simple math concept, combined with a story with easy, one-sentence reading.

Schnetzler, Pattie. *Ten Little Dinosaurs.* Two moving eyeballs, set in the book, grab the attention on every page of this hilarious rhyming counting book.

## *ComputerLink: Going Online!*

The Web is an incredible device for educators, catering as it does to a hunger for information. Kids will be turned on to what the computer is showing and not even be aware that they are reading. In fact, the Web is often like a huge information book with large pictures and small chunks of writing. We have said for years that boys would read the pictures of sports books, but they certainly gleaned a lot of information from the captions too. The same is true for the Web. You might like to consult Preston Gralla's *Online Kids: A Young Surfer's Guide to Cyberspace,* which features a suggested listing of sites to explore.

CD-ROM programs also have a great deal to offer in motivating reluctant readers to get interested in reading. Many have a lot of "bells and whistles," but the best offer a solid learning experience. *Planet Dexter's Grossology: Gross Science That Kids Want to Learn!* fascinates kids in its coverage of such "rude" topics as zits, burps, snot, spit, smelly feet and a lot more. Some other CD-ROM titles worth checking out are:

- *Earth Quest;*
- *Eyewitness Encyclopedia of Science;*
- *I Spy;*
- *Maurice Ashley Teaches Chess: For Beginners and Intermediate Players;*
- *My First Amazing World Explorer;*

- *Northern Lights: The Soccer Tails* —book by Michael Kusugak;
- *Super Solvers Gizmos and Gadgets!*;
- *Stephen Biesty's Incredible Cross-Sections Stowaway;*
- *The New Kid on the Block*—based on the book by Jack Prelutsky;
- *The Polar Express*—based on the book by Chris Van Allsburg;
- *The Silk Road;*
- *The Way Things Work*—based on the book by David Macaulay;
- *Beethoven Lives Upstairs;*
- *Up to the Himalayas;*
- *Where in the World is Carmen Sandiego?*

## AuthorLink: Joanna Cole and the Magic School Bus

School field trips were never like these!

Over ten million copies in print! A number like this assures that the author of *The Magic School Bus* series understands how to get kids interested and excited about science. Working with talented cartoonist Bruce Degen, she provides kids with jokes, amusing unexpected happenings and zesty conversation. The idea of school field trips going awry creates great delight. Cole also features concise note-taking, numerous labeled diagrams and visual asides to extend information. The cartoon format with its contrasting colors, lively action and fast pace keeps the attention of reluctant readers on the page. There is just so much to see! Create your own field trip adventures with these titles: *The Magic School Bus in the Time of the Dinosaurs; The Magic School Bus Inside a Beehive; The Magic School Bus Inside a Hurricane; The Magic School Bus Inside the Earth; The Magic School Bus Inside the Human Body.*

## KidLink: Dig a Dino

The discovery of dinosaurs has always been a source of fascination for kids, and they will listen with rapt attention to a description of the techniques used by archeologists to "unearth" the past. Try cleverly hiding artifacts, models, fossils or even a bone structure (if you have one lying around) in a special location such as a sandbox. Kids then have to figure out how to excavate these treasures without damaging them or disturbing their location. Shovels are definitely not allowed.

Look in Chapter 5 under "Claws" for many more suggested dinosaur references, but the following duo of dino kits are quite remarkable and suit this strategy perfectly:

Lambert, David. *Dinosaur! Build Your Own Model Triceratops from the Inside Out, and Discover a Lost World!* (Science Action Book). Includes all the bony parts, plus information on dinosaurs and illustrated diagrams of how to assemble.

*Presenting Leptoceratops: Book, Bones, Egg and Poster.* All the parts are cleverly contained in a plastic egg. Others contain a Brachiosaurus, Stegosaurus and a Tyrannosaurus Rex.

In contrast to the dinosaurs, the human skeleton also proves intriguing to kids. Share with them *The Bones and Skeleton Book: Get to Know Your Body from the Inside Out* and, make no bones about it, they will love assembling the foot-high skeleton from just 25 pieces.

---

*Reflection:*
Kids get so involved in whatever they are truly interested in that they forget about reading completely. They use reading unconsciously as a tool to ferret out what it is they want to find out.

---

## Record Books

The grandparent of all record books, *The Guinness Book of Records* is such a remarkable book that it should be in every classroom and home. Its perennial popularity proves that kids like facts. They want to know the biggest, the best, the longest and the most! Kids' quirky sense of humor makes them delight in the bizarre. Published each fall, the new edition is splendid with lots of photos, small chunks of information and intriguing categories, including fame, money, extraordinary people, the body, the natural world, hi-tech, war and disaster, art, music and sporting heroes. It is now also enjoyed as a television show.

Less visual and more structured than the *Guinness Book of Records*, the *World Almanac for Kids 1999* includes information about the world, complete with maps, computer terms, sports facts and entertainment, offered from an American point of view. Other general, record-type reference books include:

Ash, Russell. *The Top Ten of Everything.* Billed as the ultimate illustrated book of lists, this book includes the chicken population of the world, which country produces the most books and the worst air disasters.
Dougall, Alastair, ed. *Essential Facts.* Full of facts about the world around us, the political world, technology, science, mathematics and people.
*The Kids' Question and Answer Book.* Find out about things you've always wondered about in daily life, from goose bumps, tears, hiccuping, snoring and going bald, to facts about the animal world.

## ⟠ KidLink: The Greatest!

Challenge students to create a personal book of records in the format of a small, illustrated glossary. Ask them to identify an area of interest and to create illustrations to go along with the facts. To heighten the appeal, the category (e.g. the fastest animal) and question(s) could be put on one page, and the answer(s) on the following page. Here are a couple of possible focuses for their record books:

*WOW!*

Students select a favorite topic in a general record-type book and find pertinent facts that particularly impress them. The goal is to get a "Wow, did you know?" type of response from the kids. The topics might include food, animals or sports.

*MY BEST*

Linking to the Guinness concept, kids compile a list of their personal feats. Boasting is in! The list might include such feats as:

- the furthest I've jumped;
- the highest I've jumped;
- the longest book I've read;
- the most hot dogs I've eaten at one time.

## Sports Books

Kids love sports. They want to know who's who and what their records are. Basketball, baseball, football and hockey are all perennial favorites, and reading material must be available to accommodate these interests. Luckily, there is much available, ranging from newspaper and card sets to a wide range of magazines, information books and novels. Some sporting titles young fans will enjoy include:

Brooks, Bruce. *Cody* (The Wolfbay Wings, #3). When playing hockey, you know that "the biggest face off is yet to come ...."

Brooks, Bruce. *Zip* (The Wolfbay Wings, #2). Hockey stars think that "rage can make you great ...."

Duplacey, James. *Top Rookies* (Hockey Superstars). The best of the starters, featuring a photographic record and stats of some of the best first-season players. Highlighted by former and current stars such as Eric Lindros, Jaromir Jagr, Bobby Orr and Jean Béliveau.

Duplacey, James. *Great Goalies* (Hockey Superstars). Stop that puck! A highly visual account of some of the greatest goalies in the National Hockey League. Sections include pioneers, modern stylists, legends and playoff heroes. Favorite stars include "Felix the Cat" Potvin, Walter "Turk" Broda, Patrick Roy and Ken Dryden. See other titles: *Amazing Forwards* and *Champion Defensemen*.

Hanrahan, Brendan. *Meet the Chicago Bulls.* A glossy, action photo-packed magazine/book. Lots of stats. The glory of the game and the players is evident. Other editions are available for other teams.

Iguchi, Bryan. *The Young Snowboarder*. Simple, how-to-get-started techniques for beginning boarders.

Korman, Gordon. *The Chicken Doesn't Skate*. When a science experiment chicken turns into part-time team mascot, the team wins. But when it doesn't appear ...?

Layden, Joe. *Meet the Los Angeles Lakers*. A program-format magazine/book with lots of action photos, stats and player images.

McFarlane, Brian. *Hockey for Kids: Heroes, Tips and Facts*. A good general introduction to the sport to interest keen players.

Rossiter, Sean. *Goal Scoring*. Up-to-date strategies to show kids how to score goals. Includes what successful players such as Pavel Bure think of as their secret skills for scoring. Accompanied by many photos to illustrate points, stick skills, passing, shooting and scoring.

Smyth, Ian. *The Young Baseball Player: A Young Enthusiast's Guide to Baseball*. What you need to know about basic, defensive and offensive skills of the game. Great stop-action photos.

## AuthorLink: Matt Christopher

He shoots, he scores!

Of all the writers of sports books for kids, Matt Christopher heads the list for his ability to describe the thrill and action of the game, his knack for linking into what's in and his sheer volume of work. He writes about the action and thrill of the play in many sports, be it baseball, basketball, soccer or hockey. Christopher knows how to get kids' attention by creating appealing characters just like them, describing play-by-play action and sharing the intensity of the mood of the game. He is unique in creating characters of depth, ones with personal dimensions, such as overcoming a physical problem, a family situation or a lack of self confidence.

Christopher does not only write for older kids. He has also written a series of books which are easier to read, but have the same content and impact as his other ones. Some titles include: *Ice Magic; Shoot for the Hoop; Skateboard Tough; Snowboard Maverick; The Lucky Baseball Bat*.

## KidLink: Spotlight on Sports

Sports offer so many possible activities for involving reluctant readers in an area of great personal interest. Once we focus on their interests, we can lead them painlessly into books and related reading resources.

SLAM DUNK

One type of reading material that is extremely popular is the sports card. Encourage each reluctant reader to get the facts about a favorite player and to create a sports card. Actually, they could be subtly encouraged to make a pack of cards, including perhaps four to six of their favorite well-known sports heroes. These cards demand to be shared!

Parents and teachers can often achieve more reading goals by playing with the daily sports pages in the newspaper than with other strategies. Luckily, many newspapers now have colored photos in this section, heightening the appeal. Go with the headlines—they offer an endless motivational focus for a lively discussion of the game. Naturally, many reluctant readers will be able to discuss the game, having watched it on television: however, adults shouldn't be shy about saying "Let's see what the commentators have to say about it." When in doubt, read the section aloud to a reluctant reader and ask his/her opinion about it.

There are so many lively information articles published on all aspects of sports that it is a shame not to consult them. If interest is high for a certain player, sport or series, make a bulletin board so that many articles can be collected and shared with others and scores can be graphed. Classes can be encouraged to do their own scoring lottery and to predict the winner of special games—based on studying the statistics, of course! This forces the kids to read the sports section of the newspaper. Many already love to keep statistics of their favorite individuals or teams.

Don't forget magazines as well. It is amazing just how many are now being published. A sampling includes the following: *The Hockey News, 1998-1999 Yearbook;* The official yearbooks of the baseball teams, such as the Boston Red Sox; *The Sporting News, Hockey 1998-1999; Sports Illustrated for Kids; Transworld Skateboarding.*

## Knock, Knock! Language-Play Books

| **Play** - - - - - - - - - - - - - - - - - **Risk Taking** - - - - - - - - - - - - - - **Word Play** |
| --- |

The "best" teachers "play!" They have found that often the most successful antidote for their own boredom is to play with every aspect of language and content. We teachers are a serious lot. We are so determined that the reluctant readers in our care should gain the requisite skills to be able to read that we forget to have fun ourselves. If we don't have fun, then how can we honestly expect children to do so? Kids learn through play, but most adults have forgotten how and just work!

An easy way into reading is to play with language. We must get back to the idea of play if we are going to make a difference with the reluctant readers with whom we work. Playing with an aspect of language focuses the reader on something besides the worrying process of reading, plus it helps to lighten up learning and remove the seriousness and the need to be exactly right the first time.

There are many picture books that have been published recently that have a high degree of adult appeal because of double meaning and adult innuendo. Try Nina Laden's *The Night I Followed the Dog* and *Private I. Iguana*. Peggy Parish's books about Amelia Bedelia are hits with children because of the way in which Amelia takes her instructions literally: e.g. dust a room; dress a chicken.

Remember: if you turn literacy into work—who wants it?

## Language-Play Books

Books in which interesting language plays a major role include the following:

Betz, Adrienne. *Treasury of Quotations for Children*. A broad collection of fascinating quotes.

Christensen, Bonnie. *Rebus Riot*. Tell a story without using all the words; an introduction to the world of symbols. Codes for the rebus selections are included.

Cyrus, Kurt. *Tangle Town*. It is one of those days in a town where communication runs amuck! Blisters—blasters—plasterers: disaster in the city! Everyone goes crazy, except for a cow who escapes from her farm and saunters into this mess. Remember the old game of gossip?

Dunphy, Madeleine. *Here is the Wetland*. A vibrantly illustrated look at the animals and birds that inhabit wet places. A similarity of sentence structure, featuring "here is," "that" and "who" gives ease to the reader.

Falwell, Cathryn. *Word Wizard*. It all started with alphabet cereal and a young girl's magic spoon changing the letters around to make new words. Athough focused on young kids, older ones will enjoy the fun of such word play as ocean/canoe, stone/notes, lemons/melons and sword/words.

Feiffer, Jules. *Meanwhile* .... Uses the pattern of a stock phrase, "meanwhile back at the...," to create an amusing story about escaping a mother.

Fleming, Denise. *In the Tall, Tall Grass*. An afternoon-to-night tour through backyard grass. Easily replicated, both in text and illustration, this picture book is full of "onset" and "rime" patterns.

Folsom, Marcia and Michael. *Easy as Pie: A Guessing Game of Sayings*. An alphabetically arranged series of sayings where the letter and part of the saying are on one page and the answer on the next. For example: E—Slippery as an/eel; R—Sweet as a/rose.

Harris, Peter. *Mouse Creeps*. An easy-to-read, chain-reaction, circular story with rhyming endings on each page.

Heller, Ruth. *A Cache of Jewels and Other Collective Nouns*. Written in rhyme, this gorgeously illustrated book of nouns makes you want to start your own word collection.

Heller, Ruth. *Many Luscious Lollipops: A Book About Adjectives*. Gain the power of using descriptive words in a wonderful, asteroidal, universal, mesmerizing manner.

Hepworth, Cathi. *Bug Off!* A hilarious glossary of buggy words such as *bee*per, *smoth*ered, dyna*mite*, broom*stick*, and rom*antic*.

Jennings, Paul, Ted Greenwood and Terry Denton. *Freeze A Crowd.* Three zany Australians delight in making readers visually search for the answers to jokes and questions, all contained in hilarious illustrations. Fun for all ages!

Laden, Nina. *The Night I Followed the Dog.* When a boy sees his dog arrive home in a limo wearing a tuxedo, it's time to see where he goes!

Mathers, Petra. *Lottie's New Beach Towel.* The light-hearted romp of a chicken who receives a beach towel as a gift and goes off to the beach to use it. Hilarious word play, visual contradictions and more uses of a beach towel than you can imagine.

Most, Bernard. *There's An Ant in Anthony.* A simple amusing tale that patterns finding a small word in larger words. He did find an ant!

Parish, Peggy. *Play Ball, Amelia Bedelia.* It's baseball as you've never seen it before. What do you mean, he'll steal second base?

Park, Barbara. *Pssst! It's Me … the Bogeyman.* Vibrant illustrations, colors and print fonts highlight this flippant tale of fun and fright.

Shaw, Nancy. *Sheep in a Jeep.* Simple onset and rhyming series of books in a humorous context. Other titles include: *Sheep in a Shop, Sheep on a Ship* and *Sheep Take a Hike.*

Terban, Marvin. *Scholastic Dictionary of Idioms: More than 600 Phrases, Sayings and Expressions.* Find out about "as the crow flies," "axe to grind," "baker's dozen," "call your bluff," "dog-eat-dog world," "spill the beans" and "take the bull by the horns."

Williams, Helga. *Wordplay.* All about words: the shortest; the longest—and it isn't "supercalifragilisticexpialidocious"; fighting words; "q" words without a "u" and exotic musical words.

## *AuthorLink: Bill Peet*

Hey, I know him!

Kids know all the wonderful characters created by Bill Peet. They are just like us, getting into trouble, but most importantly, getting out of it too! Each character is so unique and has a special feeling about it. The plots, well developed with a romping sense of adventure, are very twisty, allowing for the unexpected. Bill Peet is also recognized for his love of language, having lots of fun with alliteration and rhyme. No wonder his stories read so well aloud. His wry sense of humor even allows Peet to say some serious things about the current ecological situation. Some of his titles include: *Big Bad Bruce; Chester the Worldly Pig; Fly Homer Fly; Pamela Camel; Wump World.*

⊚ *AuthorLink: Stephen Kellogg*

A world of pictures!

One look and you are caught in the exceptionally detailed illustrations and hilarious antics of Stephen Kellogg's characters. There is just so much to notice in his illustrations that reluctant readers become immersed in them and they just have to talk about them. Kellogg's work ranges from illustrating tall tales, to original stories to the many episodes of his gigantic harlequin Great Dane, Pinkerton. He is especially admired for his many tall tale titles: *Pecos Bill, Paul Bunyan, Mike Fink* and *Johnny Appleseed.*

Each page is filled with expressive watercolors, featuring a cast of thousands, all involved in incredibly expressive action. A lot of things are happening. Kellogg loves the warm affect of using golds, oranges and reds to make his illustrations even friendlier. It soon becomes apparent that one reading of a Kellogg book is not enough—there is just too much to see and enjoy again! Try one of these: *A Rose for Pinkerton; Mysterious Tadpole; Paul Bunyan; Pecos Bill; The Day Jimmy's Boa Ate the Wash; The Island Of Skogg.*

⊚ *KidLink: Word Spectrum*

Have kids create a spectrum of adjectives that can be used to describe possible reactions to some object or concept. For example, for "water":

WATER

freezing<<......cold......cool......warm......hot......>>boiling

With a word such as hamburger, as well as standard English adjectives shown below the word, the kids' current slang shown above the word, could be added in a separate sequence. For example:

radical<<......awesome......sweet......harsh......>>evil

HAMBURGER

wonderful<<......good......okay......bad......awful......>>disgusting

---

*Reflection:*

Finding the fun and idiosyncrasies in language takes the reluctant readers' focus away from their fear of trying. It helps them realize that through manipulating letters, words and phrases, there is the possibility of many right answers and a lot of fun.

---

## Alphabet Books

It used to be that alphabet books were used only in early literacy classes, but lately many more sophisticated ones have been created for older readers. Perhaps the most intriguing is Chris Van Allsburg's *The Z was Zapped*, with its "B" was badly bitten, "K" was quietly kidnapped, "N" was nailed and nailed again, and "Z" was finally zapped. It epitomizes the delight youngsters find in words, double meanings and puns, and understatement.

Alphabet books soon lead to personal dictionaries and glossaries where splendid examples of wordplay can develop. Ideas can be gleaned from the following:

Anno, Mitsumasa. *Anno's Alphabet: An Adventure in Imagination.* Make a cylinder of aluminum foil and look at the reflected images to see what is revealed.

Bayer, June. *A, My Name is ALICE.* Rhyming nonsense accompanied by hilarious and happy illustrations of animal characters selling their wares. "My name is Doris and my husband's name is Dave. We come from Denmark and we sell Dust!" What animals are they?

Birmingham, Duncan. *"M" is For Mirror.* A small paper mirror, placed just so, allows viewers to create a new image, one which reflects each word of the alphabet.

Geisert, Arthur. *Pigs from A to Z.* Seven little piglets cavort across the pages as they try to build the perfect tree house. Caught within the action, details in the copper-plate etchings include seven piglets and five forms of the letter. It's not easy to find them!

Johnson, Stephen. T. *Alphabet City.* Look carefully at the paintings of city scenes and you'll see the letters, all of which are parts of objects in our daily lives.

Joyce, Susan. *Alphabet Riddles.* Can you guess what word is illustrated and fill in the missing letters?

Maguire, Arlene. *Dinosaur Pop-up ABC.* Vibrant alphabet with lots of action scenes, even fighting. These dinos really do pop out as you turn the page.

McCurdy, Michael, illus. *The Sailor's Alphabet.* Created in the 1800s by an unknown sailor, the watercolor-tinted, scratchboard illustrations capture life on an American sailing ship.

Newfeld, Frank. *Creatures: An Alphabet for Adults and Wordly Children.* Most unusual illustrations set the tone for letters represented by Elvis, fish, Grandma Moses, Ivan the Terrible, Lincoln, Napoleon, Osiris, Pan, the Sphinx and, of course, the zebra.

Sandved, Kjell B. *The Butterfly Alphabet.* Dramatic close-up photography of butterfly or moth wings, often with the letter hidden in the intricate patterns.

Shannon, George. *Tomorrow's Alphabet.* An alphabet for solving questions based on what today's objects will turn into tomorrow.

Viorst, Judith. *The Alphabet from Z to A, with Much Confusion on the Way.* Witty romp through the quirks of the English language, similar sounding words and spellings. Accompanied by intriguing surreal images.

Whatley, Bruce and Rosie Smith. *Whatley's Quest.* An alphabet book in which the reader must search and seek to find zany details of amusing objects and words for each letter. A glossary of entries appears on the endpapers.

Wilbur, Richard. *The Disappearing Alphabet.* What would happen if the alphabet started to disappear? Twenty-six letter poems to consider.

## ⑩ *KidLink: Take a Second Look*

Start with a selection of alphabet books and have the students compare the word choice for each letter. Create a large checkerboard on one wall, assigning each square with a letter. Challenge the students to create a very individual design for each letter. Then ask them to find magazine photos, newspaper headlines, etc., with objects and words that relate to each letter. This could even go down a hallway.

Feeling quirky? Have a class that is a class from ___? Then why not challenge them by doing this activity in the reverse. Create an alphabet wall by the last letter of each word. Thus it goes: A=Victoria, B=bomb, D=surfboard, E=apple, K=book, etc.

**Palindromes**

These phrases, which read the same forward or backward, are a great delight to kids. Remember, these are difficult even for adults to think up. For example:

- A Santa at Nasa.
- Mad at Adam.
- Too Hot to Hoot.
- Madam I'm Adam!

To add challenge to the previous activity, challenge the kids to create a palindrome alphabet! Here are a few to get you started: A=abba, C=civic, D=dad, M=madam, N=noon, R=radar, S=SOS.

For help, check these books out one "noon!"

Agee, Jon. *Go Hang a Salami. I'm A Lasagna Hog and Other Palindromes.*
Agee, Jon. *So Many Dynamos! And Other Palindromes.*
Terban, Marvin. *Too Hot to Hoot: Funny Palindrome Riddles.*

## Read It Again! Books for Oral Reading

| Oral Reading - - - - - - - - - - - Fluency - - - - - - - - - - - Poetic Moments |
| --- |

A splendid means of getting reluctant students to read fluently is to encourage them to participate in playful oral readings. "Reader's theatre" is a masterful technique for achieving better oral reading. Mind you, it is important to select materials that the students enjoy and are within their reading range.

Oral interpretation, especially choral reading of any kind of literature, lets the reluctant readers hide in the crowd. Their fumbles and mistakes don't show, so they don't tighten up and become even more fearful of making mistakes. It is important though to begin this in a group of at least three so reluctant readers will have someone to rely on as a leader.

A word must be said here about "how" we as teachers and parents read aloud to kids. Reluctant readers have often been the victims of a vicious technique known as "round robin reading" or "say your mistakes aloud so others can imitate and repeat." They don't want to be caught dead reading aloud, but with patience they will sit to listen to a good reading. Thus, it is important that we read aloud so that we bring a piece of literature to life, emphasizing the meaning of the selection. Here are a few tips for successful oral reading:

- Always practice a selection aloud before reading it. Try it on you lips.
- Practice using different vocal tones for the characters. Have fun!
- Practice a variety of expressions. If you place the emphasis on one word to give the meaning, which one best deserves it? What would be the effect if you placed it on another word? Relax and enjoy.
- Practice editing the selection. Use a pencil to mark starting points and deletions. Why read "he yelled" when you can just yell? The same is true for "she sighed" when you can sigh. Often there is too much description all at once. Just edit it out. Have fun when you read aloud!
- Practice varying the rate of your reading. Which rate is most effective? When should you read more slowly for greater effect? Does high action suggest you should speed up?
- Practice varying the volume of your reading. Lowering your voice is one of the most dramatic techniques you can command to get the attention of listeners and heighten the suspense. If you want to yell—then yell! Let loose! Enjoy it! Show it!

*Reflection:*
Reading aloud to children models how wonderful a story can sound. Reluctant readers should experience reading aloud too, but never by themselves; keep them safe in a crowd.

## Poetry to Read Again

A challenge: read a poem every day!

Poetry is often neglected in the classroom, which is a shame because it can be a special help to reluctant readers who sometimes seem to have missed out on getting the rhythm and melody of our language through exposure to nursery rhymes. Because of the number of rhyming words used in our language, they can easily be used to help reluctant readers become aware of the second layer of phonics: phonograms or "sound chunks."

When you make a commitment to read a poem each day, wonderful things begin to happen. Why, the kids begin to look forward to them! Naturally, you read as expressively as you can, and always for the sheer enjoyment of saying and hearing the words. Start with funny poems that will relate to the kids, then move on to a wider range to expand their interests. Note: it is easy to sneak small poems in with other poems. Allow the kids to request favorites that have been read. Remember, it is important for the adult to enjoy the poems too; never read ones you do not like, and never, never read a poem you have not practiced on your lips. In time, you may find that the kids will volunteer to read a favorite of theirs. When this happens, rejoice! Here are some books of poems to get you started:

De Paola, Tomie. *Tomie de Paola's Book of Poems.* A collection of favorites accompanied by his distinctive watercolor paintings.

De Regniers, Beatrice Schenk, ed. *Sing a Song of Popcorn.* All kinds of poems to enjoy.

Fitch, Sheree. *There's a Mouse in My House!* If you had to exterminate a mouse, could you do it, particularly after you agreed to listen to his sad story?

Fleischman, Paul. *Joyful Noise: Poems for Two Voices.* "Buggy" poems full of rhythm and melody for solo and tandem readings.

Heidbreder, Robert. *Eenie Meenie Manitoba.* Playful read-along rhymes give an introduction to bits of Canadian culture and renowned towns.

Kennedy, X.J. *Brats.* Poems about 43 particularly outrageous kids!

Korman, Gordon and Bernice Korman. *The Last-Place Sports Poems of Jeremy Bloom.* Poems with a humorous twist by a would-be sports hero who is a constant "loser."

Lewis, J. Patrick. *Doodle Dandies: Poems That Take Shape.* Shapeshifting poetry to tantalize you, especially when its about a synchronized swim team, winter, a mirror or a skyscraper.

Lewis, J. Patrick. *The House of Boo.* A Rubaiyat type of poem, hauntingly illustrated with ghostly figures. Black backgrounds and orange print add to the spookiness.

Prelutsky, Jack, ed. *The Random House Book of Poetry.* One of the best collections of poetry to keep handy for daily use.

Sage, Allison, ed. *The Hutchinson Treasury of Children's Poetry*. A gem of a collection with superb illustrations.

Schulman, Janet, ed. *20th Century Children's Book Treasury: Celebrated Picture Books and Stories to Read Aloud*. A long-awaited collection of the best picture books and poetry to read to kids of all ages.

Silverstein, Shel. *Where the Sidewalk Ends*. A modern classic of humorous poetry for children.

Silverstein, Shel. *Falling Up*. Even more from this children's poet.

Stutson, Caroline. *By the Light of the Halloween Moon*. A cumulative poem featuring delightful repetitive phrases that make for a haunted moonlight evening.

### AuthorLink: Jack Prelutsky

Like to laugh? Enjoy funny poems? Jack Prelutsky is the poet for you. He's a talented nonsense writer whose insight into kids and the things they find amusing gives poetry a new dimension. Prelutsky is also the insightful editor of many successful collections, each with rollicking nonsense, unexpected twists and always a poem to catch our imaginations. Luckily, he includes many of his own poems to delight the reader. Starting right from his *Nightmares: Poems to Trouble Your Sleeep* book, reluctant readers have been attracted to his wacky sense of humor and love of words. His completion of Dr. Seuss's unfinished book, *Hooray for Diffendoofer Day!*, is being hailed across the continent.

Create your own poetry collection from the ones in the following books edited or written by Prelutsky:

- *The Beauty of the Beast: Poems from the Animal Kingdom;*
- *Dragons are Singing Tonight;*
- *Hurray for Diffendoofer Day!;*
- *Imagine That: Poems of Never-Was;*
- *The New Kid on the Block;*
- *Nightmares: Poems to Trouble Your Sleep;*
- *The Random House Book of Poetry.*

You can illustrate it yourself to make it extra special.

### Picture Books to Read Again

We are truly in the golden age of children's books, and nowhere can this be seen so splendidly as in the stunningly beautiful picture books being produced all over the world. Although there were so many books we would like to include, we have included only those in which the sounds and rhythms of language play a major role. Check out some of these:

Ada, Alma Flor. *Yours Truly, Goldilocks.* Red Riding Hood sends a series of letters to her friends, Goldilocks, the three pigs, her grandmother, Peter Rabbit and little bear, inviting them to a party. However, the wolves are still around!

Ballie, Allan. *Dragon Quest.* A young boy's quest to find the last living dragon. Illustrations portray both the landscape and the horrors that lay in wait throughout the journey.

Cannon, Janell. *Verdi.* A small yellow python with green stripes is sent out into the tropical rainforest to survive.

Clement, Rod. *Just Another Ordinary Day.* Amanda's real and fantasy-layered day is humorously chronicled through ordinary words and extraordinary pictures.

Cooper, Floyd. *Cumbayah.* Verses of the famous song are illustrated with singers from a variety of cultures. Some picture books just have to be sung!

Edwards, Pamela Duncan. *Four Famished Foxes and Fosdyke.* A tale of four foxes hunting and the resultant vegetarian feast. Full of "F" sounds both in text and illustration.

Emberley, Barbara. *Drummer Hoff.* Let's march in a parade! Phonogram practice in the form of a repetitive pattern text carried out with military style and precision.

Gray, Libba Moore. *Small Green Snake.* Hissing and slithering, a small green snake slides into and out of trouble. Full of chantable phrases and sss-sounds.

Knowles, Sheena. *Edward the Emu.* Bored with his life in the zoo, Edward tries one new way of life after another until he finds the right way for him. An added bonus is the rhyming endings to each line. See also *Edwina the Emu.*

Munsch, Robert. *Munschworks: The First Munsch Collection.* A collection of five of this soundster's favorites with the original illustrations by Michael Martchenko.

Sage, James. *Sassy Gracie.* A saucy maid outwits her master after she has eaten both chickens for dinner. Told with much repetition of sound-making words such as "bumpety-bump" and "clunkety-clunk."

Spurr, Elizabeth. *The Long, Long Letter.* A tall tale full of visual images and witty language, this long overdue letter brings more than news.

Winch, John. *The Old Woman Who Loved to Read.* Out on the Australian outback, the old woman loved to read and the animals knew it, surrounding her with care as she did her chores with a book in hand.

### Short Stories to Read Again

We are witnessing a resurgence of interest in the genre of the short story. This is wonderful news for reluctant readers as they get an entire story, but in a shorter form. The writers have the challenge of a scarcity of words to convey a story, depth of characterization and a sense of place. The titles below are recommended for adults to read to kids, but certainly when they get motivated by one story in the collection they may well want to try reading them on their own.

Blake, Quentin, ed. *Quentin Blake Book of Nonsense Stories.* British humor at its best, including such nonsense greats as Lewis Carroll and Edward Lear.

George, Jean Craighead. *The Tarantula in My Purse and 172 Other Wild Pets.* Shared experiences of her many favorite pets.

Mackay, Claire. *Laughs.* A collection of poems, stories and riddles guaranteed to crack a smile.

Pearson, Kit. *This Land: A Cross-Country Anthology of Canadian Fiction for Young Readers.* Features short selections from novels from each province and the north.

Schwartz, Alvin. *Gold and Silver, Silver and Gold: Tales of Hidden Treasure.* Ten tales of buried loot! True stories, legends and tall tales.

Schwartz, Alvin. *Scary Stories to Tell in the Dark.* Are you ready for these?

Simon, Seymour. *The Halloween Horror and Other Cases* (Einstein Anderson Science Detective). It's a challenge to solve these ten brainteasers.

Trelease, Jim, ed. *Hey! Listen to This: Stories to Read Aloud.* Guaranteed success with this collection. Try some nightmare short stories in chapter five.

## Longer Stories to Read Again

How fortunate we are that there are so many wonderful stories deserving to be enjoyed by kids in grades three to six. We believe that the single most important activity a teacher can do is to read aloud to kids — parents take note too! Nothing is more important or remembered longer. Nothing! The way we should undertake a novel study is by initially reading a novel aloud. This way all kids, including reluctant readers, participate in the discussions. Most importantly, the teacher becomes a fellow reader and participant.

Basically any book that you as a teacher or parent enjoy, and that is within the experience range of the kids, makes for a potentially good read-aloud. These books must be worth the time spent reading them; memorable language, rich style, fascinating characters and well structured plots are musts.

### *Favorite Read-Alouds*

The following is a list of some of our favorite read-alouds. They are not duplicated in any of the suggestions made for kids to read themselves. It was a challenge to limit this list to a few titles. The inclusion of these writers is based not just on their important novels but also on the fact that they have written so many other books that reluctant readers can enjoy.

Ahlberg, Janet and Allen. *It Was A Dark and Stormy Night.* So starts a tale of "action and absurdity, pirates, parrots and chocolate carnival cake ...."

Babbitt, Natalie. *Tuck Everlasting.* Would you really want to stay the same age for ever?

Bell, William. *Forbidden City.* What was it like to be caught in the events surrounding Beijing's Tiananmen square massacre?

Cooper, Susan. *The Boggart.* Caught in a computer, a Scottish type of hobgoblin does not like coming to Toronto to live, and so seeks his revenge.

Creech, Sharon. *Walk Two Moons.* A long car ride across the states with her grandparents gives Salamance a chance to try to bring her mother back home. She does—but not the way she thought.

George, Jean Craighead. *Julie of the Wolves.* Lost on the tundra, a teenager survives with the help of a wolf pack.

Gleitzman, Morris. *Blabber Mouth.* An amusing and poignant account of the difficulties facing Rowena in a new school because she can't talk due to a birth defect.

Jennings, Paul. *Unreal!* Eight stories from Australia's favorite kids' writer.

Lewis, C.S. *The Lion, the Witch and the Wardrobe.* What happens when you go through into the land of Narnia?

Lowry, Lois. *The Giver.* Is a futuristic world as great as it sounds? Jonas, who at twelve, goes into training to be the next Receiver of Memory, begins to have serious doubts.

MacLachlan, Patricia. *Sarah, Plain and Tall.* Imagine getting a mother by mail order! A family on the prairies works it out.

Naylor, Phyllis Reynolds. *Shiloh.* A boy's love for a dog overcomes all.

Richler, Mordecai. *Jacob Two-Two Meets the Hooded Fang.* This kid has to say everything twice to get attention, but when in a dream he is put in a prison, he proves his worth.

White, E.B. *Charlotte's Web.* Just in case you missed this classic about the relationship between a runt of a pig and a spider.

### Audiobooks

Kids are tuned in!

A major development in recent years is the appeal of taped books, or as *Publisher's Weekly* refers to it—audio fiction. These are a blessing for blind individuals, but now with leading actors reading the text and background sound effects to heighten the effect, the appeal is for all of us. Long a domain of long distance truck drivers, whose interest in Louis L'Amour novels is legendary, this media is coming into its own. Public librarians in some branches report that taped books are the leading circulation item for young adults, beating out paperback novels. One family living in Prince George held regular discussions prior to the long drive—8+ hours—to Vancouver for the spring break. Which books would they listen to? They planned for two down and two back. Kids and parents each got to select a story they wanted to hear. What a wonderful way to make a trip go faster!

Some taped books you might enjoy include the following:

- Coville, Bruce. *The Ghost in the Big Brass Bed.* Read by Christina Moore (4.7 hours).
- Cushman, Karen. *Catherine Called Birdy.* Performance by Kate Maberly (3 hours).
- Dahl, Roald. *Matilda.* Read by Ron Keith (5.25 hours).
- Fleischman, Paul. *Joyful Noise: Poems for Two Voices* (3 hours).
- Hobbs, Will. *Beardance.* Narrated by George Guidall (5.5 hours). Also *Bearstone.*
- Jacques, Brian. *Redwall.* Narrated by Ron Keith (20 hours).
- Jacques, Brian. *Redwall.* Performance with 23 voices by Brian Jacques (11 hours).
- O'Dell, Scott. *Island of the Blue Dolphins.* Performance by Tantoo Cardinal.
- Paterson, Katherine. *Bridge to Terabithia.* Read by Tom Stechschulte (4 hours).
- Paterson, Katherine. *The Great Gilly Hopkins.* Read by Alyssa Bresnahan (4.75 hours).
- Paulsen, Gary. *Gary Paulsen World of Adventure: Skydive!* Narrated by Jeff Woodman (1 hour).
- Taylor, Theodore. *The Cay.* Performance by Levar Burton (1.75 hours).
- Yolen, Jane. *Wizard's Hall.* Read by the author (3 hours).

*KidLink: Taped Books*

In this strategy, reluctant readers get the chance to prepare a tape for younger readers. Having to read an "easy book" on tape for a younger audience and all the practice involved in reading it perfectly, helps get these kids over the fear of reading aloud. A further step would be to have two or three reluctant readers work together, reading only one part each and adding sound effects. Even though taping requires repetitious practice, they almost look forward to the taping sessions. They especially like doing ghost and haunted house stories at Halloween. Fortunately, scary stories are "in" all year long.

# And Then ... the Story Takes Over! Caught up in the Action!

Story - - - - - - - - - - - - - - Image - - - - - - - - - - - - Dreadful-to-Sublime

How easy it is for kids to get caught up in the action of a good story. We see it as kids tell each another about their weekend adventures. After a trip, they have a lot to talk about, and this form of storytelling certainly involves both teller and listener.

Kids today have been raised in a visual world, what with the impact of television and glossy magazines. It is not much of a surprise then that they often prefer a visual form of story. It allows them the ease of knowledge while talking about it with their peers.

The media also plays an important role in leading kids into the world of print. In this section, we begin with movies and videos, then go on to the most visual kinds of books: wordless books; picture books for older readers; series and chapter books from easier to more difficult; "cool" books; "good reads" including comics and graphic novels; and, finally, finish the section with the Web.

## Visual Stories

### Movies

The appeal of movies for kids is bigger than ever, thanks in part to the multi-million dollar budgets spent on promotion of each title. Companies want to create as much hype as possible to boost movie attendance, for the box office counts, as well as the potential video rentals and sales. Such super hype creates interest in reluctant readers, primarily because their peers are caught in this web of intrigue and they want to be part of it, to be seen as part of the crowd. Also, many adults around them are talking about the movies, perhaps even going with them to view the latest. This cross-generational appeal provides lots of people to talk to, and reluctant readers like to talk!

It cannot be denied that regardless of how Disney rewrites a good story, the magic wand of Disney creates a major financial success. Disney has a vast organization for marketing its movies, and more importantly, a vast merchandising wing for creating peripheral products that link up to the movies. Thus, we have seen for the movie *Mulan:* coffee mugs, T-shirts, pendants, action toys and, of course, the Disney version of the book, which, as is often the case, is much different than the original. Robert San Souci's *The Legend of Fa Mulan* picture book, dramatically illustrated by Jean and Mou-Sien Tseng, is a terse retelling of the famous tale, yet a good one to share with reluctant readers because their interest in the movie version is already high.

What we adults, teachers and parents, need to remember is that Disney provides us with a guaranteed successful way in to reading with reluctant readers. Go with the kids! Go with what the kids are interested in at this moment. Disney helps to make their entry into books so much easier.

Other movies that have had high interest with reluctant readers are, of course, *Jurassic Park* and *Star Wars*. "In" movies change constantly and demand that we—parents and teachers—have to work to keep current.

## Videos

Kids of this generation have grown up with videos in a variety of formats: games, stories, movies, etc. Often having been babysat by them when their parents wanted some quiet time with friends, many kids will talk about regularly having fallen asleep while watching one.

Even commercial video games such as *Final Fantasy VII* offer reading opportunities in a palatable version for reluctant readers. In this game, the players must read instructions to create characters in the game. Reading the dialogue between characters leads to the next opportunity to score. They also have to read directions on other ways of scoring and the means of getting to harder levels. Finally, they read their score sheets. This game is so engrossing that it will literally keep kids going for days! Some videos that are worth viewing include:

- *Amazing Grace*. Based on the book by Mary Hoffman.
- *The BFG*. Adapted by John Hambly. Based on the book by Roald Dahl.
- *The Fool of the World and the Flying Ship*. Based on the book by Arthur Ransome.
- *James and the Giant Peach*. Based on the book by Roald Dahl.
- *Johann's Gift to Christmas*. Based on the book by Jack Richards.
- *Linnea in Monet's Garden*. Based on the book by Leena Anderson and Christiana Bjork.
- *The Mouse and the Motorcycle*. Based on the book by Beverly Cleary.
- *The Story of Rosy Dock*. Based on the book by Jeannie Baker.
- *The Sweater*. Based on the book *The Hockey Sweater* by Roch Carrier.
- *Where the Forest Meets the Sea*. Based on the book by Jeannie Baker.

## Wordless Books

The major appeal of wordless books is that, by having limited or no words, they provide youngsters with an opportunity to talk about a story and create their own plot. Since these books tell a story exclusively through the illustrations, reluctant readers don't get hung up on the recognition of the words. Some, such as John Goodall's *English Village*, simply invite the readers to experience the historical changes in a specific location. Examples of wordless books evidencing complexity of detail of illustration and of story include the following:

Anno, Mitsumasa. *Anno's Journey.* Hundreds of folk-tale characters can be found in this European journey.

Baker, Jeannie. *Window.* As we look through a window along with a growing boy, we see the changes in a community.

Banyai, Istvan. *Zoom.* A series of scenes, with a boy and a girl looking at a rooster, but each continues to get further away.

Briggs, Raymond. *The Snowman.* In comic book format, a young boy's snowman comes to life and he invites the snowy fellow into his house to see his world.

Collington, Peter. *A Small Miracle.* A woman, living on the street, experiences a personal epiphany with a crèche scene at Christmas.

Day, Alexandra. *Good Dog, Carl.* Left to watch the baby, the Rottweiler has a wonderful adventure with the child, yet the grown-ups never figure it out.

De Paola, Tomie. *Pancakes for Breakfast.* Talk about making pancakes from scratch! This old lady knows all about it.

Mayer, Mercer. *Frog Goes to Dinner.* Amusing slapstick fun when a boy's friend, his frog, goes along to a restaurant in the boy's pocket.

McCully, Emily A. *Picnic.* An outing in the country is interrupted when it is time to eat. The mouse family realizes the youngest one is missing and has fallen off the truck. She causes trouble in *School* too!

Spier, Peter. *Noah's Ark.* Two by two, the animals enter one of the most crowded ships imaginable. Filled with a myriad details and varying-sized illustrations, there is much to see and talk about.

Spier, Peter. *Peter Spier's Rain.* What fun! A brother and sister enjoy a rainy, windy day. What are puddles for anyway?

Turkle, Brinton. *Deep in the Forest.* An amusing variant of the three bears, only this time it is the baby bear that wreaks havoc!

Wiesner, David. *Tuesday.* This was the day when the invasion of frogs began!

Weitzman, Jacqueline Preiss. *You Can't Take a Balloon into the Metropolitan Museum.* A delightfully clever and uproariously funny wordless adventure told on two levels. A little girl goes to the art gallery with her grandmother and is informed by the guard that she can't take her balloon inside. He ties it to a handrail and indicates that he will look after it. While they enjoy the museum's paintings, he pursues the balloon after a bird unties it.

### KidLink: Wordless Books Brought to Life

Why not buy two copies of a wordless title and laminate each page of one copy to create a series of pictures? Students can then arrange them in an order that would make a story. Actually, the discussion of the order of illustrations is most valuable, as it evolves a sense of story. Of course, you may also wish to encourage students to write out the story, even different versions, on large charts or maybe prepare a taped version with sound effects.

### Highly Visual Picture Books for Older Readers

A dramatic revolution has taken place in the picture book field. Long thought of as a genre only for young preschool children, many titles are now being created for older readers. Every picture book has different levels of meaning and, in many, the level of sophistication has risen sharply. Many of them are aimed at the adult buyer, stressing their aesthetic appeal or their clever adult wit and humor. The concepts and time references in these books are quite demanding. Kids like complexity too and this is evident in a book such as Grahame Base's *Animalia*. In double-page spreads, this book visually captivates the reader by the prolification of objects, starting with the letters of the alphabet. That lounging lion in the littered library is not alone!

When kids look at a book differently than an adult does, it is because kids today are more highly visual than previous generations, thanks—or no thanks—to the impact of television and computer games on their lives. These kids prove to be good at reading pictures, an important coping skill that can be used by reluctant readers to infer plot and characters. It appears that the illustrations make reading the words easier. Here are a variety of sophisticated, highly visual picture books your older reluctant readers might enjoy:

Baker, Jeannie. *The Story of Rosy Dock.* The devastating spread of a non-native plant across Australia, highlighted by amazingly detailed collages.

Baker, Jeannie. *Where the Forest Meets the Sea.* Remarkable collages show a father and his son viewing the rainforest in northern Queensland, but questioning its survival in the future.

Bodkin, Odds. *The Crane Wife.* Exceptionally detailed illustrations bring to life the traditional Japanese tale of a beautiful young girl who marries a poor sailmaker and then makes wondrous cloth for him.

Briggs, Raymond. *The Man.* A unique friendship between a boy and a seven-inch man, told in typical Briggsian style—a cross between cartoon and novel.

Browne, Anthony. *Willy the Wimp.* A puny kid gorilla trains to become a "he" man in his attempt to overcome the neighborhood bullies and impress his girlfriend, Millie.

Bunting. Eve. *Train to Somewhere.* A young orphan girl leaves New York to find her mother. At the last stop, she realizes her mother will never be there and so she stays with an older couple who adopt her.

Coerr, Eleanor. *Sadako.* The pictorial retelling of the novel *Sadako and the Thousand Paper Cranes.* A young girl, dying from the effects of the atomic bomb, believes she will get better if she can just fold 1,000 paper cranes.

Crew, Gary. *The Watertower.* Two boys climb the tower in an outback Australian town during the summer drought to go swimming. Evocative illustrations.

Granfield, Linda. *In Flanders Fields: The Story of the Poem by John McCrae.* A Canadian surgeon wrote this famous poem about the first World War on the battlefield as he took a break from his work in a field hospital.

Hathorn, Libby. *Way Home.* A homeless boy befriends a small kitten.

Howe, James. *I Wish I Were a Butterfly.* We can wish our lives away unless we realize that others see us as desirable.

Innocenti Roberto. *Rose Blanche.* The turn of events in the war as seen through the eyes of a young German girl.

Jackson, Ellen. *Turn of the Century.* A clever walk though history, featuring a boy or girl's story of their life at the beginning of each of the ten centuries prior to the new millennium. Ornately detailed paintings give additional facts and a sense of the time period.

Keens-Douglas, Richardo. *Freedom Child of the Sea.* A slave ship crashes and slaves are released, some to the watery depths.

Kroeger, Mary Kay and Louise Borden. *Paperboy.* At the time of the 1927 historic fight between Gene Tunney and Jack Dempsey, a young boy sells newspapers to help his family.

Laden, Nina. *Private I. Iguana: The Case of the Missing Chameleon.* Hilarious account of a lizard in distress. The work of this private eye is done with much word play, visual puns and quirky humor.

Laden, Nina. *When Pigasso met Mootisse.* A hilarious word play on the works of Henri Matisse and Pablo Picasso as two artists, a pig and a bull, have a verbal fight. Building and painting a fence between their houses actually creates an artistic masterpiece, bringing them back together as friends.

Levine, Arthur A. *Pearl Moscowitz's Last Stand.* As the years go by, the culture and neighbors change, but Pearl stays. When the city wants to cut down the ginko trees, it is time for Pearl to make her last stand.

Louie, Ai-Ling. *Yeh Shen: A Cinderella Story from China.* Exquisitely illustrated by Ed Young with impressionistic images within the shapes of fish.

Maruki, Toshi. *Hiroshima No Pika.* Dramatic impressionistic view of the devastation of the bombing on a young girl's family.

Mollel, Tolowa M. *The Orphan Boy.* A Masai account of the story of the evening star, in which a young boy comes to stay in the village until an old man becomes curious about his special powers.

Morimoto, Junko. *My Hiroshima.* Photos and drawings highlight the author's experience of being a young girl at the time of the bombing.

Oberman, Sheldon. *The Always Prayer Shawl.* As was the family tradition, Grandfather Adam gave his grandson, Adam, the family prayer shawl as he told him the heritage surrounding it.

Polacco, Patricia. *Pink and Say.* True story of two boys fighting for the Union in the American Civil War; Pinkus saved Sheldon, but in the end both were captured. Pinkus, being black, was hanged.

Van Allsburg, Chris. *Polar Express.* What are the holidays without a trip North to visit Santa?

Van Allsburg, Chris. *Two Bad Ants.* As this duo explore the kitchen, they give us an insectal view of breakfast. Gross!

Yolen, Jane. *The Girl Who Loved the Wind.* A Chinese princess, protected from all unpleasantness by a high palace wall, hears the wind sing and spreads her cape to see the world for herself.

Young, Ed. *Lon Po Po: A Red Riding Hood Story from China.* Subtle images of the wolf haunt each page, but the trio of girls thwarts his hungry intentions.

Young, Ed. *Seven Blind Mice: An Indian Fable.* How is it possible for seven small creatures to describe something as big as an elephant? Each takes a part and describes it to the other—a strange composite of an image results.

Zeman, Ludmila. *Gilgamesh the King.* One of the world's oldest stories, originally written on clay tablets, is stunningly illustrated in the style of Middle Eastern reliefs and tablets.

## AuthorLink: Patricia Polacco

This is my story. Babushka is my mother!—When one thinks of an author/illustrator who has a story of her own to tell, we immediately think of Patricia Polacco. In her books, she shares her Ukrainian heritage with young readers, including the warmth of family love and support. Each book is made memorable by her delight in color, composition, facial expression and intriguing details in the clothing and her famous Easter eggs. We just have so much to look at that her works become a memorable read. One characteristic in her books, as with Polacco herself, is a firm belief in hope. Things will be better and we can make them so. She has, and so can we!

A recent book, *Thank You, Mr. Falker,* is Polacco's way of thanking her grade seven teacher, who discovered that she was "dyslexic" and that this was the cause of her reading problems. She was exceptional in her art ability but could not read. He spent time privately with her after school until she could achieve success. Now she combines both talents to our delight in such titles as: *Chicken Sunday; Pink and Say; Rachenka's Eggs; The Keeping Quilt.*

### Chapter-Type Books—Series That Are Worth Reading

Many of us enjoy books that are in a series. If we like one book in the series, it is likely we will enjoy others. The familiarity of the writing style also provides a safe escape. Each volume follows a pattern; the vocabulary, the action and the characters are basically the same for each book. A reluctant reader, in particular, doesn't have to spend energy on figuring out new people; the struggle to read is eased. This accounts for the appeal of such books as Enid Blyton's "adventure" series, as well as Franklin W. Dixon's "The Hardy Boys" series, and Carolyn Keene's "Nancy Drew" series, which now have updated versions. Books in a series provide an emotional connection to the characters; we know who they are and how they are going to act.

Often, reluctant readers get startled with uncertainty while reading a book in a series , yet we must not underestimate the power of peer pressure to make them determined to conquer a book. Frequently all kids in the classroom are reading the current fad series. These short "cool" books are often chapter books with short chapters, lots of white space between lines and several black-and-white or colored illustrations.

Such series allow reluctant readers to relate to their peers on a level they previously could not. At a literary/academic level they can't relate, but with common story, language, plot and common experience, they can talk story and be accepted as equals. This is precisely what happened with the "Goosebumps" series published by Scholastic. These books quickly became the "hot" read of the English-speaking world. R. L. Stine told the kids they were going to be scared and they were! Each fast-paced, dialogue-filled chapter was embedded with a magnificent hook at the end, making readers "just have to" find out something in the next one. The books are still around, but their popularity has rapidly diminished. Scholastic has now encouraged R.L. Stine to write for an older age group in an attempt to gain a greater share of the market.

Another appealing series is the "Animorphs" by K.A. Applegate, in which a group of kids fight alien interference. The action is fast paced and the suspense is killing. Each book is focused on one of the characters and the pressure on them to successfully achieve their mission. The characters must morph themselves into other forms. This is the exciting part, as, with only slight discomfort, various central characters become a gorilla, lobster, rhino, bat, spider, butterfly, and in one of the latest, a cobra. This later book is so designed that a reader can flip the edges and actually see the boy turn into the cobra. Because of the popularity of the "Animorphs" series, Scholastic has created "Megamorphs." Titles such as *In the Time of the Dinosaurs* are part of this series made longer to keep the action continuing and the suspense ongoing.

Some of the current pop-culture series are frankly just junk, but for reluctant readers they set up a level of desire to read in order to be "in" with their peers. Frequently, once these children learn to read better, they will progress to better books because when they can read adequately, they will show the same discrimination as other regular readers. As a grade seven boy told Mary, "If I hadn't started to read Goosebumps in grade five, I would not be a reader today!"

There are many levels of difficulty for chapter books in series that can be successfully managed by kids. Many publishers identify series books by a set of levels, focusing on the reading levels ranging from preschool to grade four. Since each publisher's designated levels may be slightly different, we must establish our own criteria. Always remember that interest in a topic means kids will read at a higher level. We have arranged our recommended titles in four sections, going from easier to harder.

## I Can Read These

Although the books in these series tend to be primary looking, they are also quite fun to look at and easy to read. Many of the titles at this level of reading are well written but some are quickly done and superficial, hence each needs to be reviewed for quality. Never depend on just the series name! Some titles include:

Bauer, Marion. *Allison's Wings* (Hyperion Chapters). Wanting to fly, Alison tries out outfits such as a cape and a pair of feathered wings before she finds her own answer.

Buck, Nola. *Creepy Crawly Critters: And Other Halloween Tongue Twisters.* Octoberian groans and howls will result from a reading of these spooky plays on language.

Cole, Joanne. *Monster Manners* (Hellow Readers!). An out-of-step monster child tries her parents with her strange manners.

Davis, Lee. *Dinosaur Dinners* (Eyewitness Readers). Primary-reading-level account of what dinos eat.

Ehrlich, Fred. *Lunch Boxes* (Puffin Easy-to-Read). A day in the life of a school lunchroom and what happens to the food once the children are there.

Hooks, William. *Lo-Jack and the Pirates* (Bank Street Ready-to-Read). A kidnapped cabin boy's misunderstanding of orders has hilarious results.

Jewell, Nancy. *Silly Times with Two Silly Trolls* (An I Can Read Book). Five short episodes with a pair of funny, forgetful trolls.

Maestro, Marco and Giulio. *What Do You Hear When Cows Sing? And Other Silly Riddles* (An I Can Read Book). Be prepared to groan at the humor of these bullish language plays.

Novak, Matt. *Newt* (An I Can Read Book). Describes the antics of a swamp-living salamander.

Rylant, Cynthia. *Henry and Mudge: The First Book.* Some friendships are made to last. *Henry and Mudge Get the Shivers* and a dozen others continue the series.

Skofield, James. *Detective Dinosaur Lost and Found* (An I Can Read Book). Oops, detectives are not supposed to get lost in the dark!

Smith, Janice Lee. *Wizard and Wart in Trouble* (An I Can Read Book). A pet vulture tells the wizard and his dog that trouble is coming; preparations are made to meet it!

Spirn, Michele Sobel. *The Know-Nothings* (An I Can Read Book). A quartet of friends who cannot figure out what to eat.

Vaughan, Marcia. *Goldsworthy and Mort: In Spring Soup* (A Ready, Set, Read Book). Two friends make soup together, one clam chowder, the other baked bean hot pot—all in the same pot.

## These Look Like Chapter Books

Although they are relatively easy to read, the titles in these series have more of the look of books with real chapters. If a reading level is not officially given on the cover, an examination of length of story, length of sentence, vocabulary, number of lines on the page and size of print will give you an approximate level appropriate for the child.

Brown, Marc. *Arthur Makes the Team* (Arthur Chapter Books, #3). After Arthur joins little league the big question is if he will get to play. *Arthur and the Crunch Cereal Contest* is also part of the series.

Cosby, Bill. *The Meanest Thing to Say* (Little Bill Books for Beginning Readers). "So?"—a great word to counteract any mean thing said to you!

Croll, Carolyn. *Too Many Babas* (An I Can Read Book). It's a case of too many grandmothers for the soup!

Himmelman, John. *The Animal Rescue Club* (An I Can Read Chapter Book). Four friends are out to help animals in trouble.

Levinson, Nancy Smiler. *Snowshoe Thompson* (An I Can Read Book). Based on a historical figure who gives a young boy help in crossing over a mountain on homemade cross-country skis.

Parish, Peggy. *Play Ball, Amelia Bedelia* (An I Can Read Book). Never have you seen baseball played like this! In another title, *Come Back, Amelia Bedelia*, misunderstandings leave her new job in a mess.

Royston, Angela. *Fire Fighter!* (Know It All Readers). The alarm sounds and we follow along to the fire!

Sharmat, Marjorie Weinman. *Nate the Great and the Missing Key* (Nate the Great). A young detective full of short, terse, Sam Spade-like (adult movie detective) dialogue and exaggerated tongue-in-cheek humor.

Wilkinson, Philip. *Spacebusters: The Race to the Moon* (Eyewitness Readers). Photos of American and Russian crews add credibility to the first lunar landing.

Yolen, Jane. *Commander Toad and the Intergalactic Spy* (Commander Toad). Out on a search for one of the most wanted spies—his cousin!

## I Want to Read These

Many older reluctant readers want to read stuff that looks like what the other kids are reading; it doesn't have to be as hard, it just has to "look" the same. Ann M. Martin's books in the series "The BabySitter's Club" have certainly made an impact with girls in many classrooms. Want some more sure bets? Try these:

Amato, Carol. *Captain Jim and the Killer Whales* (Young Readers' Series). Full of fascinating facts about killer whales and other creatures in their lives.

Arthur, Robert. *The Mystery of the Green Ghost* (The Three Investigators). As the ghost oozes through the wall, he leads the trio to a coffin where the skeleton is wearing the Chinese ghost pearls. In another title, *The Mystery of the Whispering Mummy*, a 3,000 year old mummy suddenly begins to whisper strange words.

Calmenson, Stephanie and Joanna Cole. *The Gator Girls: Rockin' Reptiles* (Beech Tree Chapter Books). A new gator in town upsets Allie and Amy's friendship.

Dadey, Debbie and Marcia Jones. *Hercules Doesn't Pull Teeth* (The Adventures of the Bailey School Kids, #30). Four kids who live in Bailey City ask themselves if the new dentist, who has huge muscles, could really be Hercules?

Donnelly, Judy. *The Titanic Lost ... and Found* (STEP into Reading). The story of the sinking of this famous vessel and the search for it in the ocean depths.

Donnelly, Judy. *True-Life Treasure Hunts* (STEP into Reading). A series of adventures in locating hidden treasure.

Greenburg, Dan. *Never Trust a Cat Who Wears Earrings* (The Zack Files). Weird things happen when Zack is scratched by an Egyptian cat statue that has come to life. Great, he starts to turn into a cat!

Haskins, Lori. *Breakout! Escape from Alcatraz* (STEP into Reading). Three men try to break away from the famous San Francisco bay prison.

Karr, Kathleen. *The Lighthouse Mermaid* (Hyperion Chapters). During a storm, Kate has to help in a rescue—could it really be a mermaid?

Larson, Kirby. *Sitting in a Tree* (Cody and Quinn). The friendship of a boy and girl is upset when the neighborhood bully teases them about kissing.

Levy, Elizabeth. *Frankenstein Moves in on the Fourth Floor* (A Trophy Chapter Book). Sam and Robert think that their new neighbor must be a monster.

Little, Emily. *The Trojan House: How the Greeks Won the War* (STEP into Reading). How a cunning plan by the Greeks ended a ten-year war.

Osborne, Mary Pope. *Pirates Past Noon* (A Stepping Stone Book: Magic Tree House, #4). Jack and Annie look at a book in the tree house and are transported to an island just as a motley crew of pirates arrive to seek hidden treasure.

Pascal, Francine. *No Escape!* (Sweet Valley Twins, #118). How long can these girls survive anyway? The junior version of Sweet Valley High made especially for young girls.

Paulsen, Gary. *Amos Goes Bananas* (Culpepper Adventures). A gorilla falls in love with Amos!

Roy, Ron. *The Canary Caper* (A Stepping Stone Book: A to Z Mysteries). Just as the circus comes to town, pets start to disappear. After they are returned by strangers, the owners' homes are robbed.

Shea, George. *Amazing Rescues* (STEP into Reading). Three hair-raising tales of daring and danger.

### I'm Hooked on These

Older female students are very peer conscious when they graduate from Francine Pascal's "Sweet Valley Twins." They need something to go to. Obviously, "Sweet Valley High" is one possibility, but there certainly are others from which to select. Boys will often move from "Goosebumps" to "Animorphs," or directly into darker horror or adventure books. Here are some titles that might be appealing:

Brooks, Bruce. *Billy* (The Wolfbay Wings, #7). In hockey we find that "being the best is not enough ...."

Conrad, Pam. *Staying Nine* (A Trophy Chapter Book). Heather thinks that nine is just the perfect age—why get older?

George, Twig C. *A Dolphin Named Bob* (A Trophy Chapter Book). A mischievous performing dolphin keeps aquarium audiences in suspense.

Leverich, Kathleen. *Best Enemies Forever*. Former friends cause sparks when they try to outdo each other. Felicity acts as if she is a star and can't stand the competition of Priscilla, who has started a new volunteer service club—Ordinary Little People. Another title is *Best Enemies*.

Levithan, David. *In the Eye of the Tornado* (Disaster Zone Books). Fact and fiction about being caught in the eye of the storm.

Levithan, David. *In the Heart of the Quake* (Disaster Zone Books). As the pressure under the earth start to build up, two brothers try to locate its site before the quake strikes.

Levy, Elizabeth. *Dracula Is a Pain in the Neck* (A Trophy Chapter Book). Could the real Dracula be haunting the boy's summer camp?

Martin, Les. *Ghost in the Machine* (The X Files, #11). Agents Mulder and Scully track the killer of a computer company's CEO while tracking down an evil computer virus.

Scieszka, Jon. *Tut, Tut* (The Time Warp Trio). Taken back in time to ancient Egypt, our heros try to outwit an evil priest, but can their boy-king friend help them? Other titles include *Knights of the Kitchen Table*, *2095* and *Your Mother Was a Neanderthal*.

Wilson, Eric. *Escape from Big Muddy*. Tom and Liz Austin get involved in kidnapping and biker gangs on a road trip through Saskatchewan. Others titles include *Code Red at the Supermall* and *Disneyland Hostage*.

---

*Reflection:*
Series books are repetitive in word and action, a subtle kind of practice, yet exciting and "in." They stimulate that most important ingredient for reluctant readers—desire to read.

---

### "Cool" Books

There is tremendous pressure on kids to be part of their peer group; to be "cool." Thus, we need to watch out for what is "in" in the kid-culture scene, keeping a constant eye on the media and other kids. Often the books they read are an expression of their rebellion against life—the more outlandish the better. This could be said to be the major appeal of the "Goosebumps" series. We once heard a young boy in a bookstore turn to his dad and say, "Daddy, I want something really cool!"

The only constant in this area is change. Tastes change and so do the reading demands of kids.

A remarkably "cool" series is Brain Jacques's *Redwall* series. Boys from ten to twelve years of age are lost in these books. Reluctant readers in grades five and six, who want to be seen as "cool," struggle through the writing style, with its archaic English, challenging names and complex characters. On the other hand, they are completely absorbed in the fantasy of good versus evil.

A twelve-year-old friend of Ron commented: "I like Redwall books because they have good plots, yet the writing is difficult to read and the books are four hundred pages long. They are interesting because the bad guys are rats, ferrets and weasels, while the good guys are mice, squirrels, badgers, moles and rabbits. I like how they make a cute, cuddly mouse play the part of a bloodthirsty rebel trying to save his people. The characters are well done, especially the evil Rat Lord trying to take over a peaceful town of animals, or a rebel that will die before surrendering. If you like bloody battles without seeing blood spewing out of somebody's body, read a Redwall book!" A few of the titles include:

- *Mossflower;*
- *Outcast of Redwall: A Tale from Redwall;*
- *Redwall.*

With the revival of *Star Wars*, more of its books are becoming popular again. Reluctant readers might enjoy some of these:

- Anderson, Kevin J. and Rebecca Moesta. *Star Wars Young Jedi Knights: Diversity Alliance.*
- Golden, Christopher. *Return of the Jedi* (Choose Your Own Star Wars Adventure).
- Golden, Christopher. *The Empire Strikes Back* (Choose Your Own Star Wars Adventure).
- Reynolds, David West. *Star Wars: The Visual Dictionary.*
- Reynolds, David West. *Star Wars: Incredible Cross-Sections.*
- Windham, Ryder. *Star Wars: Battle of the Bounty Hunters.*

Finally, these three miscellaneous "cool" titles hold almost universal appeal for reluctant readers:

Pilkey, Dav. *The Adventures of Captain Underpants.* Two kids convince their school principal that, dressed only in a cape and little else, he can overcome crime.

Oppel, Kenneth. *Silverwing.* Follow the flight of a young bat as he tries to rejoin his colony on its southward migration.

Farmer, Nancy. *The Ear, the Eye and the Arm.* Set in Zimbabwe in 2194, a trio of mutant detectives try to find three kidnapped kids.

### KidLink: "Zines" Are Too Cool!

Magazines are always cool.

Largely due to their high-gloss photographic appeal, almost everyone is attracted to magazines, as is evident at newsstands, at airports and in the large chain bookstores. As you travel on a trip or to work, look around and see what people are reading—usually newspapers, paperbacks and a host of magazines. As adults, we like the appeal of being able to start reading anything that grabs our interest and only to read as much as we feel like. The same is true for reluctant readers. Introduce them to some of these popular "zines" for kids:

- *16 Magazine;*
- *BOP;*
- *Game Buyer;*
- *Game Pro;*
- *Model Airplane;*
- *Motorcyclist;*
- *Nintendo Power;*
- *Seventeen;*
- *Sports Illustrated for Kids;*
- *Teen;*
- *Teen Beat;*
- *Teen Machine;*
- *Teen People;*
- *Word Up* (music);
- WWF (World Wrestling Federation).

**Lost in a Good Book**

There comes a time in life when everyone discovers a really good book, and, once involved in the story, they do not want to be disturbed. What the book is depends on the reader. Kids need to have the delicious experience of getting lost in a book. This is one of the serendipitous moments in the life of a reluctant reader and a most joyous one for the teacher or parent. Mind you, don't blow it by being too enthusiastic, for reading is an individual delight—or a secret sin!

### *Bug Off! I'm Reading!*

It takes a special book to reach younger reluctant readers, but when one does, kids get quite overwhelmed by the experience. Not that they will make a fuss about it; no, they must remain "cool" with their friends. But, they do talk about the book for a long time. The challenge for adults will be to figure out what the next book will be and in which direction the kids will be going. Here are a few that might work:

Banks, Lynne Reid. *Harry the Poisonous Centipede: A Story to Make You Squirm.* Harry is poisonous but shy! A highly illustrated account of his daring and brave adventures.

Bunting, Eve. *Nasty, Stinky Sneakers.* Who will win the school's smelliest sneaker contest?

Cleary, Beverly. *Runaway Ralph.* The friendship of a boy and a mouse who has his own motorbike.

Coville, Bruce and Katherine. *Sarah's Unicorn.* Sarah's witchy aunt is trying to get Sarah's special friend.

Rubin, Jim. *Porkchop to the Rescue* (Doug Chronicles). Doug and his Scout brothers go camping but get lost in the dark forest. Hooray for his dog Porkchop who saves them.

### Caught in the Grip!

There is another group of reluctant readers who are older and can read, but are not turned on. They do not find reading enjoyable and need to be motivated to realize what it is like to be caught in the grip of a good story. When was the last time you realized you couldn't put a book down?

There is almost an overabundance of exciting books available; the challenge is how do kids, teachers and parents find out about them? Start with the school library and the public library as both have trained individuals who like to read and often provide lists of good titles. Teachers might like to get Charlotte Huck's *Children's Literature in the Elementary School*, a text frequently used in children's literature courses, for their school. Specialized texts, such as Ron Jobe's *Cultural Connections,* also contain reading lists. Don't underestimate the power of word-of-mouth; if you read a good book you just have to share it. Remember, a good story is a good story no matter what grade level.

Our suggestions are not exclusive as there are so many good books available. We wanted to recommend certain authors whose books are especially appealing to reluctant readers. As we have already included over 1,000 titles in this book, we have purposely kept the following section much shorter than it might otherwise be.

Coville, Bruce. *Aliens Ate My Homework.* Fast-paced, hilarious account of strange aliens who need help to fix their spacecraft.
Korman, Gordon. *The Zucchini Warriors.* MacDonald Hall abounds with action when the school's football team gets sponsored by a company selling fried zucchini sticks.
Lowry, Lois. *The Giver.* A future society in which kids grow up without choices; they are selected for jobs. All seems well, until Jonas decides to leave.
Naylor, Phyllis Reynolds. *Shiloh Season.* Did you ever wonder what happened to Shiloh?

### Comics

There can be no doubt that reluctant readers are into comics. It is the format and the fast pace of the story that keep them reading and trading them with their friends. What is popular? Russell Ash in *The Top Ten of Everything* listed three comic writers as the best-selling children's authors in the world. René Goscinny and Albert Uderzo have sold over 250,000,000 copies of titles from their "Asterix the Gaul" series since the first one appeared in 1959. Georges Remi, who writes under the pen name of Hergé, has sold over 160,000,000 copies of titles from his "Tintin" series since 1948.

Newbery Award-winning writer Jerry Spinelli, in his autobiography *Knots in My Yo-Yo String*, shares that as a kid he did not read novels. He was a cereal box reader and read comics by the hundreds. With a good background of comic books, reluctant readers are ready to either just keep reading them or to go on to novels that make use of the cartoon format. Some comic possibilities include the following:

* *The Adventures of Tin Tin* by Hergé;
* *Archie;*
* *Asterix* by R. Goscinny & A. Uderzo;
* *Batman;*
* *Calvin and Hobbes* by B. Watterson;
* *The Far Side* by Gary Larson;
* *Garfield* by J. Davis;
* *Spiderman;*
* *Superman;*
* *X Men.*

## Graphic Novels

Graphic novels are on the cutting edge of writing experimentation. Some of them are meant for older teens and adults, but they all have a dominant visual component. To get to the "edge," give these titles a try to see if they capture the kids' attention. You'll note a wide variety in intensity of illustration and reading level.

Feiffer, Jules. *A Barrel of Laughs, A Vale of Tears.* A rollicking medieval Knight's tale with a shapeshifting prince, a lady in distress and a disgruntled author. Black-and-white drawings "expand" the text.

Octon, Henni and Elizabeth Honey. *45 + 47 Stella Street and Everything That Happened.* A twelve year old writes about how a group of kids try to expose a new couple in the neighborhood who they call the phonies and think are criminals.

Pilkey, Dav. *The Adventures of Captain Underpants.* Imagine the school principal being conned into thinking he is going to save society wearing only a cape and his ???

Older kids will enjoy these:

Avi. *City of Light, City of Dark: A Comic-Book Novel.* Two friends must keep a mysterious token safe and away from the woman who is desperate for it.

Morrison, Grant. *Batman Gothic.* Our hero is in classic form in this tale.

Spiegelman, Art. *Maus, A Survivor's Tale: My Father Bleeds History.* A powerful glimpse of what happened to the Jewish people in World War Two: in this story, the Jews are mice and the oppressors are cats.

Veitch, Tom. *Star Wars: Dark Empire II*. Follow the adventures of the Star Wars crew.

## The Web Takes Over

Kids are surfing the Web! The Web has so much to offer that at times it appears quite mind boggling. Any topic reluctant readers can think of can be found at some site. Sites full of facts, detail and exotic information related to all possible interests are there for the finding. We need to learn to "bookmark" those sites that are particularly outstanding. When kids have the will and freedom to just play on the Web, they don't seem to be bothered about being lost in cyberspace.

### *Literary Web Sites*

There are great sites out in cyberspace related to literature, kids and reading. One of the best is the David Brown site from the University of Calgary found at: *http://www.ucalgary.ca/~dkbrown/index.html*. He has created what is considered to be the leading site linking to other sites. Rich in lists featuring many topics and awards from several countries, it serves as a central station for hundreds of sites on all aspects of children's literature. Another site is that of the American Library Association at *http://www.ala.org/alsc*. This is the organization that gives out such prestigious awards as the Caldecott, Newbery, Batchelder and Wilder medals. It also has lists of the best and notable books of each year, as well as the "Quick Pick" for reluctant readers.

Other impressive sites are the ones done by the following individuals or organizations:

- Banned Books at *http://www.cs.cmu.edu/People/spok/most-banned.html*
- The Bulletin of the Center for Children's Books at
  *http://www3.sympatico.ca/ccbc/mainpage.htm*
- The Canadian Children's Book Centre at *http://www.Iglobal.com/~ccbc/*
- Canadian Society of Children's Authors, Illustrators and Performers (CANSCAIP) at *http://www.interlog.com/-canscaip/home.html*
- Carol Hurst at *www.carolhurst.com/*
- Children's Literature: Beyond Basals at
  *http://www.poky.srv.net/~gale/beyondbasals.html*
- *Family PC* at *http://www.familypc.com*
- Jim Trelease at *http://trelease-on-reading.com/*
- Internet Public Library's Literary Criticism at
  *http://www.ipl.org/ref/litcrit/*
- Kay Vandergrift at *www.scils.rutgers.edu/special/kay/kayhp2.html*
- Nancy Polette Online at *http://www.nancypolette.com/hom.htm*

- National Library of Canada's list of Canadian authors and illustrators of books for children and young adults at *http://www.nlc-bnc.ca/services/ekidauth.htm*
- Publishers Weekly Interactive Web Page at *http://www.bookwire.com/pw/childrens.articles*
- The Society of Children's Book Writers and Illustrators (U.S.) at *http:// www.scbwi.org/*
- Susie Wilde's Once Upon a Lap at *http://wildes.home.mindspring.com/*

Teachers and kids can look up these special interest sites to find titles of great books listed in the bibliographies they contain. Caution: there is no guarantee of the quality nor the accuracy of these lists! Anyone can, and does, post lists. Double check your findings.

*Series Sites*

There are many sites that have a strong literary interest for kids, perhaps based on their favorite series. Try the following:

- Arthur: *http://www.pbs.org/wgbh/pages/arthur/*
- BabySitter's Club: *http://scholastic.com/BabySittersClub*
- Dav Pilkey: *http://www.pilkey.com/*
- Goosebumps: *http://scholastic.com/Goosebumps*
- Magic School Bus: *http//scholastic.com/MagicSchoolBus*
- Sweet Valley High: *http://www.sweetvalley.com*
- Where's Waldo?: *www.FindWaldo.com*

*Publishers' Sites*

When kids spot that their favorite books come from one publisher, they may want to find out what other titles the company has produced. This gets them actively involved in seeking out titles and authors. Most of these companies have impressive sites to explore. Need we say, teachers will enjoy this activity too? Consult the following:

- Allen & Unwin: *www.allen-unwin.com.au*
- Bantam Doubleday Dell: *www.bdd.com/teachers/*
- Dorling Kindersley: *http://www.dk.com*
- Harcourt Brace: *http://www.harcourtbrace.com*
- HarperCollins: *http://www.harpercollins.com/kids/*
- Houghton Mifflin: *www.hmco.com/hmcom/trade/childrens/index.html*
- North South: *www.northsouth.com/*
- Scholastic: *www.scholastic.com* (Canada) *www.scholastic.ca* (Australia) *www.scholastic.com.au*

### Author Sites

"Hey, let's look up our favorite writer!"

Surfing the Web has great appeal for some reluctant readers. Using the Web to find the home page of their favorite author or illustrator is another way to keep them actively involved. We have listed a select number of Web sites, but with the reliability of search engines, all you need to do is to type in the author's name and sites will appear—some that may surprise you!

- Arnold, Caroline: *http://www.geocities.com/Athens/1264*
- Brett, Jan: *http://www.janbrett.com/*
- Carle, Eric: *http://www.eric-carle.com/*
- Kropp, Paul: *http:www.do.com/~author/*
- L'Engle, Madeleine: *http://www.geocities.com/Athens/Acropolis/8838/*
- Paterson, Katherine: *http: //www.terabithia.com/*

---

*Reflection:*

While surfing the Web may seem like play to reluctant readers and not look like reading to us, in fact, using computers, CD-ROMs and the Web requires a great deal of reading. Consider it a new kind of book, one to browse and skip around in but still full of words, both easy and esoteric. A lovely sneaky sideswipe!

---

# 5 ∗ Go with the Kids!
## Interest Entry Points

*In today ... out tomorrow!*

One never knows what will capture and excite the imagination of kids since they are so strongly influenced by the media and their peer group. Mind you, many kids do have very individualistic interests and some rugged topics seem to stick around forever. A few of these perennial favorites include: disasters, cars, the ridiculous and dinosaurs. Facts, such as those contained in the Guinness Book of Records, are forever appealing, even to adults.

Go with the kids! One way to turn kids on is to listen for and discover their current interests. Even when we think we know, reluctant readers will frequently hide their real interests behind something they say is appealing. They may tell us they are interested in sports when they really could care less. These kids are hiders. They are afraid and expect to fail again! We must develop a very aware ear and eye to be able to ferret out the subtle hints that let us know what truly interests them.

It is a good idea to have reluctant readers go to the school library, and yet, they are afraid of libraries too! We need to conduct tours and direct these kids to something specific. They need a good clear focus: "Today we are going to find books on dinosaurs." If we know their real interests, we can take them to the appropriate section and "expect" them to physically pull the books off the shelf and peer inside.

Kids need to learn how to browse. Somehow reluctant readers don't think they are allowed to or that they know how. Whether it be in a library or a bookstore, the process of browsing needs to be informally talked about. We all need freedom to wander through the shelves, take journeys of discovery between the covers or just peruse one book. Parents or teachers should not be censors. Allow all materials to be available to kids. Let's not forget that many teachers and parents need to learn how to browse too! Why not do it together? Maybe you will all have wonderful serendipitous finds.

In the following sections, we share examples of a variety of interest entry points that catch the attention of many reluctant readers enough for them to want to read. We have selected six interest fields from many possible ones in order to provide a diversity of topics and a multiplicity of entry points. One way we have entered some interest fields is via a link such as a "KidLink" or an "AuthorLink." Each link within a topic gives teachers and parents an opportunity to connect specific children and specific interests to many resources. Whether or not the topic is of interest to the child will ultimately depend on that child's perspective. Don't force these or any topic on any reluctant reader.

## The Dark Zone!

Most of us are fascinated, whether we like to admit it or not, by the horrible things in our lives—real or imaginary. Some children do face a range of horrible situations in their daily survival: desertion, abuse, bullies, gangs, drugs, killings and living on the streets. For others, it is their nightmares, fears of unknown things in their closets or under their beds, or strange insects. Other imaginative youngsters create aliens, vampires and monsters in their daily lives.

Is horror too frightening for youngsters? For most, not at all. They see their peers reading such books and there is an overabundance of scary movies and ads on television. What adults have to remember is that children view horror in their terms, not through adult eyes. Remember that with books, youngsters have the power to stop the horror by simply closing the cover! Television does not work this way though, as rarely do we click for a channel change, staying mesmerized by the violence and killings.

The following web illustrates a range of topics related to horror that could be used as directions to explore and motivate reluctant readers. These are suggestions only and can be developed further by assembling many reading resources to entice readers.

Nightmares
  Caught
  Chases
  Car crashes, falls
  Kidnapped
  Killings, drownings

Creepy places
  Haunted houses
  Spooky dark places
  Dank glades

School
  Teacher questions
  Print in books
    Too small/too much
    Long sentences

War
  Bombs and bombing
  Guns

# THE DARK ZONE

Beastly creatures
  Bugs/insects
  Snakes
  Spiders

Horror in our lives
  Bullies, gangs
  Homelessness
  Abuse
  Desertion
  Drugs
  Street kids
  Murder, death
  Unsuspecting victims

Worthlessness of humans
  Unmindfulness of others
  Becoming a robot

**Black, Blood, Beasts**

Disasters-Natural
  Crashes
  Explosions

Out of this world
  Outer space
  Science fiction

Fears and phobias
  Goosebumps
  Unsolved mysteries
  Vampires, werewolves
  Transformations
  Animorphs
  Technology gone astray

## The "Goosebumps" Phenomenon

A fairly recent craze affecting most youngsters is Scholastic's "Goosebumps" series. Walk into any classroom and the children will readily tell you about a Goosebumps book. Competent readers soon tire of the books, which they say are boring and repetitious. Reluctant readers keep reading them because they are comfortably repetitious and they can gain great prestige in the classroom as they too are reading what their peers are—none of that baby stuff anymore.

R.L. Stine has crafted a clever formula for children. He places great emphasis on plot, tells readers how they will be frightened and astutely places a hook at the end of each short chapter to encourage the reading of the next one.

Have you ever dreamt of being someone or something else? Kids have fertile imaginations and many of them enter a fantasy world of make-believe characters at the drop of a hat. Imagine viewing the world through the eyes of a lobster. Don't get excited; they are evidently very short sighted! This is the appeal of K.A. Applegate's *Animorphs*, another current series of titles highly popular with youngsters.

⑨ *KidLink: Change Yourself for a New Perspective*

Take time to have the children tell you what they like about these books. It is important for reluctant readers to be seen reading them, and by taking an interest in them, teachers are modeling that reading, while important in our lives, can also be fun. Teachers "must" read at least one or two titles, just to be aware of the "joys" found in them. Be aware that an emerging trend is a diminishing interest in these titles and be alert for the next craze. Your reluctant readers will want to read from the new ones too.

Beyond Goosebumps? Horror is the stuff of many movies and television series. It is not surprising then that quite a few youngsters graduate to the more horrific titles by adult writers of this genre, including: Stephen King, Clive Barker, Michael Crichton, Anne Rice, John Saul and Dean R. Koontz. If you want some tales at their level to give them nightmares, read some of these:

Brown, Marc. *Scared Silly! A Book for the Brave: Poems, Riddles, Jokes, Stories and More.* You have to be brave to read this chilling collection.

Leach, Maria. *Whistle in the Graveyard: Folktales to Chill Your Bones.* It is amazing what can happen in a two-page story.

Lunn, Janet, ed. *The Unseen: Scary Stories.* Spooky poems and stories to haunt an evening's reading; guaranteed to capture your interest.

McKissack, Patricia C. *The Dark-Thirty: Southern Tales of the Supernatural.* Be prepared for what comes out of the dark!

Pepper, Dennis. *The Oxford Book of Scary Tales.* A collection of some of the best stories to haunt your reading.

Powling, Chris, ed. *The Kingfisher Book of Scary Stories.* Don't read these ten tales at night or in a dark room!

Prelutsky, Jack. *Nightmares: Poems to Trouble Your Sleep.* Rapidly becoming a classic as these poems of ghouls, skeletons and haunted houses remain popular with kids.

San Souci, Robert. *More Short and Shivery: Thirty Terrifying Tales.* You might be afraid to read these!

## Beastly Creatures

Never underestimate the power of horrible-looking creatures to capture the attention of youngsters. Horrible to some, engrossing to others. Plain "gross" to a few adults!
Need we mention slugs, spiders, snakes and more?

### *KidLink: Bat Fever*

In a summer school class, the teacher had planned and structured a series of lessons on interesting places across the country. One child happened to say, "I saw a bat last night!" The others replied, "No kidding!"—and there was no way the planned events of study were going to get done. Luckily, the teacher was inventive and soon the entire class was absorbed in looking for books about bats: bat poets, bat facts, bat photos and even bat sounds.

If bat fever strikes, quickly share Janell Cannon's *Stellaluna*. It is the vivid account of a young fruit bat who gets separated from her mother. She learns a lot in her attempt to survive. A small plush toy of Stellaluna is also available to cuddle while reading the book in bed!

One of the most engrossing bat fantasies is Kenneth Oppell's *Silverwing*. In this story, a young silverwing bat gets lost in a storm on the annual southern migration. He meets a brightwing bat and together the two friends attempt to catch up with the colony. Naturally, strong forces of evil are present in the form of two gigantic, flesh-eating tropical bats, with wing spans of over six feet. This is an excellent read-aloud and the fantasy in the book itself keeps older reluctant readers glued to the pages. Some other books to bat an eyelash include the following:

Appelt, Kathi. *Bat Jamboree.* A counting book featuring 55 bats performing a wing-flapping review at an old drive-in theatre.
Arnold, Caroline. *Bat.* Fascinating close-up photos of the night flyers.
Danziger, Paula. *There's a Bat in Bunk Five.* An insecure girl longs to get away from her family, but camping with giggling girls 24 hours a day is not her idea of a good time.
Gilson, Jamie. *It Goes Eeeeeeeeeeee!* A new kid tries to scare the other boys about bats, but is put in his place by a girl who has a couple of them living in her garage.
Johnson, Sylvia A. *Bats.* Dark shapes glide on silent wings! These are not frightening creatures, but very beneficial.

## ∞ *KidLink: Go Bugs!*

Kids are fascinated with all sorts and sizes of bugs. Just have a beetle cross the floor, a spider spin a web, or a wasp buzz around, and there is a guaranteed audience. The secret is to turn this interest into reading. Gather books together that tell about the bugs that have entered their lives.

We've seen that when a teacher has been able to obtain an enormous Brazilian cockroach for the classroom, she claims instant attention. Gross? Not really, just fascinating for every one! Kids will readily return the next day to check on their specimen. Naturally, references will have to be consulted. These huge cockroaches will give you the opportunity to talk about their care and also the features of domestic cockroaches—their tenacity and their danger as carriers of disease.

How can you get rid of cockroaches and other pests? This question could lead to research on extermination strategies for getting rid of termites, fleas on pets, head lice and other "beasty" problems.

Bugs in your own house? If you are lucky, intriguing bugs will be serendipitously found. Start a visual "Bug Collector's" bulletin board, where kids can sketch the bugs they have located in their street or community. Design a "Bug Collector's" badge to wear. You need to get out and capture some bugs too!

Here are some buggy books you might just like to read:

Boniface, William. *Mystery in Bugtown.* A pair of moveable eyeballs follow the antics of Inspector Cricket as he tries to solve the case. Information on bugs included at the back.

Brenner, Barbara. *Thinking About Ants.* Simple text with rave illustrations detailing life underground.

Else, George. *Insects and Spiders* (The Nature Company Discovery Library). Large close-up glimpses of insect senses, sight and defenses.

Greenaway, Theresa. *The Really Hairy Scary Spider and Other Creatures with Lots of Legs.* Featured sections include hairy hunters, fast movers, clever disguises, ant attack, tiny tanks and beastly bugs.

Hepworth, Cathi. *Bug Off!* A hilarious glossary of buggy words such as *bee*per, *smoth*ered, dyna*mite*, broom*stick* and rom*antic*.

Imes, Rick. *Incredible Bugs: An Eye-Opening Guide to the Amazing World of Insects.* Extensive close-up photos of all aspects of insects and their daily lives.

Llewellyn, Claire. *The Best Book of Bugs.* A luxuriously illustrated look at spiders, ants and a honeybee's year.

Tomb, Howard and Dennis Kunkel. *MicroAliens: Dazzling Journeys with an Electron Microscope.* Challenging writing with black-and-white photos of up-close ugliness— the horror of bugs, water creatures, bacteria and humans.

*Totally Amazing Spiders.* Fabulous close-up photos show spiders as they really are. Bright breezy snippets of text on eye-catching pages are filled with intriguing information.

## Kidnapped!

A horrible fear for many children is the danger of being abducted or kidnapped. Newspaper columnists are quick to extol the dangers in every community. Is it much wonder that mothers grow paranoid and a sense of fear creeps into the lives of children?

A lively discussion could ensue as to just how a young child could be kidnapped from the playground or shopping mall; who, why, when? How can parents and older siblings safety-proof them to prevent such a happening?

### AuthorLink: Caroline Cooney

Caroline Cooney writes with refreshing frankness about what kids face in their lives, crafts a well-developed plot, evokes crisp dialogue and raises such intriguing questions in the minds of the characters that readers become totally fascinated by them. She guarantees that there will be lots of talk during the reading of her books.

Cooney's remarkably powerful novel, *Face on the Milk Carton*, will captivate the students. What is it like to be a 13-year-old girl who, at lunch time at school, stares at a photo of her younger self on a missing poster on a milk carton? Who are her real parents? How did it happen? The power of this story will make kids want to find out. When she goes to meet her "real" family in *Whatever Happened to Janie?* many more questions are raised. Is blood really thicker than water?

### A Living Horror

Many kids face horror of a different type in their daily lives: abuse, alcoholism, drugs or family violence. It is impossible to detect the amount of abuse—physical, verbal or sexual—faced by kids. Is it any wonder why so many kids exude such thick skins? The horror may be faced in the classroom too: an oppressive teacher, a class bully or the uncertain adjustment of an immigrant child. In Australian writer Diana Kidd's *Onion Tears*, a young Vietnamese girl faces a hard adjustment period. Nam Hong does not speak at school, having been so traumatized by her last days in Vietnam and the killing of her family. Only when an understanding teacher gets ill do the words begin to flow. Except for the swallows returning south, the action could be anywhere in North America.

### AuthorLink: Eve Bunting

... yet there is always hope in our endeavors.

One of the most thought-provoking writers of pictures books for kids about challenging life circumstances is Eve Bunting. Her secret is to immediately engross the reader in unfamiliar situations. Once caught, she develops the characters through dialogue and understatement to a point where each reader cares about the characters and their plights. Fortunately, her editors have paired her with talented artists who have extended and developed the characters and stories. Each of her books focuses on a poignant situation in the life of someone, enabling reluctant readers to walk in others' shoes for just a short while. Adults will have much to relate to too, as a good story is one for many age levels! Eve Bunting loves words and this is certainly evident in all her works, picture books or novels. Some of her titles include: *A Day's Work; Fly Away Home; How Many Days to America: A Thanksgiving Story; Smoky Night; The Wall; Your Move.*

### The Horror of War

Many kids are caught in a war zone. Ask elementary boys about war and words such as guns, bombs, planes and landmines explode forth. Kids are fascinated by conflict. Is it any wonder, with the major television networks bringing far-flung conflicts into our living rooms on a daily basis, that kids become jaded and almost comatose to the impact of killings and bombings? Combined with the daily violence witnessed in crime adventure series on television, in which an astounding number of people are killed, kids today are passive viewers of some very violent fare. Can we really expect them to understand the concept of peace?

We believe that the best anti-war strategy is to read students a good war novel. When a novel such as Lois Lowry's *Number the Stars* is read, kids become aware of the human elements involved; characters facing hard times, fear, starvation and death. All people in a war zone, especially the kids, are affected by the conflict. Perhaps, after reading such a novel, readers can more fully appreciate where they live and why it is important that peace be obtained.

Fortunately for reluctant readers, there have been several powerfully-written picture books about war that are focused on older readers. Roberto Innocenti's *Rose Blanche* depicts the impact of World War Two on a small town in southern Germany. All is upbeat and celebratory as young Rose Blanche watches the incredible detail of the troops massing for war. Later, when the first wounded soldiers begin arriving, the mood changes. One night she witnesses truckloads of children being driven through her town. She follows and finds a concentration camp at the end of the forest. She shares her food with some of the children there. As the tide of the war changes and people flee the advancing American troops, she goes for one last visit to see the children, but the camp is gone—only a fog enshrouded clearing is there—then a shot rings out!

Junko Morimoto's *My Hiroshima* gives a personal experience of the August 6, 1945 bombing, with photos and poignant illustrations. It is a very moving account and can be compared to Toshi Maruki's *Hiroshima No Pika*, where a young girl and her family are eating breakfast when the flash comes. Expressionist illustrations convey the pain, suffering and horror of the event. Eleanor Coerr's short book, *Sadako and the Thousand Paper Cranes*, is the story of a young girl, who even though she folded nearly 1,000 paper cranes, died of leukemia as a result of the bombing. Coerr rewrote this into a picture book, *Sadako*, with haunting illustrations by Ed Young.

Patricia Polacco's *Pink and Say*, another compelling story, is a true story of two boys fighting for the Union in the American Civil War. Pinkus saved Sheldon, but in the end they were captured. Pinkus, being black, was hanged.

**Disaster Strikes!**

For some unfathomable reason, students are fascinated with disasters—be they natural or human-made.

The story of the Titanic heads the list, and 12:30 a.m. on April 15, 1912, is forever etched in the minds of the young. The Titanic has become the twentieth century's most dramatic symbol of disaster and has given rise to hundreds of collectibles: pictures, mugs, spoons, T-shirts, videos and, of course, books. The best-selling movie and video certainly have spawned much interest in the many books available.

Hurricanes, tornadoes, typhoons, landslides, earthquakes and floods are impressive forces of nature that also fascinate youngsters. That fascination is heightened by television news coverage of such disasters brought immediately into our homes as they happen.

From a distance, some disasters are rather funny. A reading of Chris Van Allsburg's picture book *Jumanji* will provoke a sense of awe, as well as gales of laughter and delight. The game fascinates the audience and it proves to be even better than the movie—although it must be admitted that certain special effects in that were spectacular.

Some disaster-related titles that might intrigue include:

Bonson, Richard and Richard Platt. *Disaster! Catastrophes That Shook the World.* This book includes a collection of disasters: historical, weather-related and human-made.

Ducy, K. and K.A. Bale. *Survival, The Titanic, April 14, 1912.* Gavin is working in the galley to pay for his passage to America when the crash happens.

Levithan, David. *In the Eye of the Tornado* (Disaster Zone Books). Fact and fiction of being caught in the eye of the storm.

Levithan, David. *In the Heart of the Quake* (Disaster Zone Books). What it is like to be caught in a real shakeup!

Marschall, Ken. *Inside the Titanic: A Giant Cutaway Book*. Double page fold-outs offer cutaway views of the inside of the ship.

Platt, Richard. *Stephen Biesty's Incredible Explosions: Exploded Views of Astonishing Things*. Incredibly detailed views of a space station, Antarctic base, windmill, airport and human body, as well as the Grand Canyon and Tower Bridge.

Tanaka, Shelley. *The Buried City of Pompeii: What It Was Like When Vesuvius Exploded*. Fascinating illustrations portray the action of people caught in this tragic event.

Tanaka, Shelly. *On Board the Titanic*. Photos, illustrations and split text show the structure of the ship and the location of people.

## Really "Hot" Wheels!

Kids want action! They are fascinated with movement—something that they can actually do, to get involved, and move. They want to see action shots in the books and magazines they look at. There are kids who, after they tear something apart, can put it back together again. Some even start from scratch, building from the ground up.

One such young reluctant reader wanted a mountain bike in the worst way but his family had no money to buy one. He did have a paper route and began saving. Finding a bicycle frame one day while doing his paper route was what really got him started. Each piece he needed had to be researched thoroughly in catalogues, manuals and on the Web. A decision then had to be reached about what kind of part it was he needed. He searched through newspaper want ads, the local sports shop ad boards, garage sales, police sales and sports shop clearance sales until he found what he needed and could afford. Little by little, over two years he worked, constantly consulting many sources of information and cleaning, painting and greasing—putting together his dream. Now he looks longingly at sports cars!

Kids want to move! Having a car is often referred to as "having wheels" by older teens. For younger reluctant readers, having wheels might be owning a bike, a skateboard or roller blades. The point is to get places faster. As travel agents often state, "getting there is half the fun!" The web on the opposite page gives some ideas of where this interest can lead.

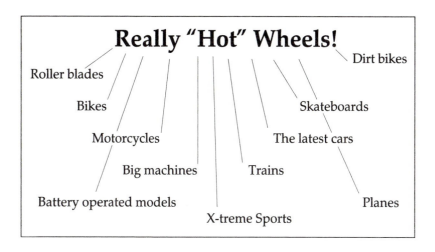

## Really "Hot" Wheels!

Roller blades

Bikes

Motorcycles

Big machines

Battery operated models

X-treme Sports

Trains

The latest cars

Skateboards

Dirt bikes

Planes

Here, also, are some "hot" books to get things rollin':

Allen, Bob. *All Action Mountain Biking*. An introduction to beginning aspects of this sport, with many tips for successful riding experiences. Other titles include *Mountain Biking* and *Skateboarding*.

Awan, Shaila, ed. *Monster Machines*. An easy-to-read description of some of the biggest, heaviest and chunkiest machines that can move.

Bingham, Caroline. *Big Rig* (Mighty Machines). Short and easily read, with large print and great photos of these impressive rigs. See also: *Race Car*.

Butterfield, Moira. *Record Breakers* (Look Inside Cross-Sections). View the interiors of many speed machines.

Christopher, Matt. *Dirt Bike Race*. The question everyone is asking around the track is "Is Ron's luck about to run out?"

Christopher, Matt. *Dirt Bike Runaway*. A genius at fixing bikes, Peter runs into danger when he takes off from home.

Cleary, Beverly. *Lucky Chuck*. Simple account of a boy riding his new motorbike too fast. Super endpapers with bike illustrations.

Delton, Judy. *Pee Wee Scouts: Pedal Power*. A bike ride proves very eventful for a young boy.

Godfrey, Martin. *Here She Is—Ms. Teeny Wonderful*. She's got a conflict between being a dirt biker or a beauty queen!

Graham, Ian. *How It Goes: Racing Cars*. Find out about current technology, engines, design, racing rules and tactics for car racing.

Harvey, Ian. *Tanks* (Look Inside Cross-Sections). Prepare to be amazed at the detailed illustrations revealing what is really inside one of these monster machines.

Llewellyn, Claire. *Tractor* (Mighty Machines). Short and easily read, with large print and great photos. See also: *Truck*.

Parker, Steve. *Making Tracks: Explore the World of Land Machines From Bikes to Bulldozers*. A simply written but highly visual look at the workings of these machines.

Somerville, Louisa. *Rescue Vehicles* (Look Inside Cross-Sections). Highly detailed illustrations, short snippets of text and a myriad facts.

Sutton, Richard. *Car* (Eyewitness Books). The history and workings of cars, from horseless carriages to modern models.

Turnbull, Andy with Debora Pearson. *My Arctic Adventure: By Truck to the North.* Drive 5,000 miles (8,045 km) with Bill Rutherford on his 18-wheel big rig, all the way from Vancouver, through northern British Columbia and the Yukon, and over the Arctic ice road to Tuktoyaktuk.

Tuxworth, Nicola. *Let's Look at Things That Go.* Extra-easy text snippets accompany photos of many vehicles.

*The Visual Dictionary of Cars* (Eye Witness Visual Dictionaries). A multitude of labels focus your attention to all the bits and pieces.

Wilson, Anthony. *Visual Timeline of Transportation.* How we've transported things through the ages.

## Crazy about Cars

Kids all know about Mattel's remarkable line of toy cars. These are most impressive, as they are dye-cast, made of metal, have rubber tires and come in a variety of colors. Their quality of reproduction is admired by all ages; many adults collect these accurate models too. There is an incredible range to be found: Winston Cup cars, Indy cars, CART cars, fantasy cars such as the Batmobile and the Viper, cartoon cars, dragsters, and even fire trucks. What's also great about them is their impressive catalogue about all the models available.

Many kids are interested in the latest models of cars and keep track of new developments. Check out the following magazines: *Car Craft; Four Wheeler; Hot Rod; Hot Rodding.*

### KidLink: Museum of Cars

All kids enjoy sharing their prized possessions, especially if others don't have the same. Create a class "Famous Car Museum" by encouraging the kids to bring in their car models from home. All museum items must be described with a label in front of them. Thus, kids have to read to get the information and then present it in a brief and appealing manner on the card. They will be able to get the necessary information by referring to Mattel's "Hot Wheels" catalogue and reference books.

### KidLink: Car Racing

If kids are passionate about car racing, they are passionate! They will follow the big three circuits: Winston Cup, Indy and Grand Prix, Formula One Races. Kids might be lucky enough to see an actual Indy Series race, particularly if they are close to any of the sites of the 19 races: Vancouver; Toronto; Palm Beach; Detroit; Lexington, Ohio or Fontana, California.

If they cannot see an actual race, videos are readily available of all the races, particularly of the most important car race of the year, the Indianapolis 500 Race. Have kids prepare a documentary of part of the video, acting as the announcer and pointing out major facts to their classmates.

As in any field, car racing has its own terms, which kids could explain. Some of these include the following: checkered flag; green flag; open-wheeled cars; pace car; pace up; paddock; refueled; retired; the pits; tire walls; yellow flag; RPM—revolutions per minute.

The technology of car racing is awesome at the very least! Ask the kids to talk about what types of technology they are seeing. For example, you will notice that in each driver's helmet there is a two-way radio that connects him with the team manager and that the car has a live-action camera facing down the track. This signal is beamed above to a hovering helicopter, which deflects it to a trailer parked in the paddock and then relays it to the television station for public viewing.

**On the Go!**

Wheeled devices of all types hold great appeal for many reluctant readers. They often have a passionate interest in the latest models of bikes, skateboards, roller blades and other "hot wheels." Magazines to whet the reluctant appetite include: *Bicycling; Cycle World; Mountain Bike; Motor Cyclist; Sports Illustrated for Kids; Transworld Skateboarding.*

*KidLink: Rollin' On ...*

The following three activities highlight the strategy of getting reluctant readers relating to various types of wheels through "user-friendly" resources.

*SKATEBOARDING*

Everywhere you go, you are certain to find kids practicing on their skateboards. It is a very positive activity, as the individuals try to increase their skill level with more difficult maneuvers. What are these? Checking out the magazine *Skateboarding* will give you some idea of what they are doing, as will watching various sports channels that broadcast skateboard events. This is one sport that has yet to have really appealing books for reluctant readers.

The following are some tricks that you can watch for and that reluctant readers can illustrate and describe to their classmates: 360 Kickflip; Shove-it Kickflip; Frontside 180 Kickflip; Backside 180 Kickflip; Frontside 360 Ollie; Ollie Impossible; Feeble Grind; Crooked Grind; Frontside Nosegrind; Backside Tail Slide. If you can obtain a video, the kids may wish to give their own commentary describing the action of the skate-boarders.

MODELS

If you aren't big enough to have the real thing, then maybe a model will do in the meantime. Kids likely cannot have that racing car or 18-wheel truck, but they can have a model of their favorite wheeled device. One reluctant reader was so captivated by the idea of putting together a model of his favorite sports car that he read everything on the outside and the inside of the model kit box, including all the directions for assembling the car. Not surprising, in the classroom he insisted that he could not read and would never attempt to read anything remotely related to school subjects. When another boy got interested in the model as it was being assembled, they got into great debates about whether it was being done correctly. Obviously, they would refer back to the directions. The reading level of instructions for models ranges from quite easy to quite intricate with detailed instructions using very technical vocabulary. Reluctant readers can progress in their reading ability through just reading model instructions.

### HOW-TO RESOURCES

Keeping up with interested kids in the area of "really 'hot' wheels" requires a very resourceful parent or teacher who will help to locate the many how-to books that are available. Kids want to know how to build, how to repair and how to design. Reading instructions for model kits can be helpful. Check out your local bookstore, newsstand, model store, bike dealership or public library for other suitable how-to materials.

Kids may wish to share operating instructions for things they already own—bikes, skateboards or roller blades—or wish they had—Lamborghinis, Beamers and Harley "Hogs." Invite them to compare the manuals for various models and companies. Have one of the students explain the manual to others who do not have the model.

To extend this, set a problem and have the kids figure out how to fix it, always consulting the manual.

## Girl Power!

Girls are said to read stories with appealing characters and interactions. Some do, but others are more interested in action and how the world around them works.

Over the years, Pippi Longstocking has been a popular figure; the girl who went to school for one day so that she could enjoy the holidays. As well, Anne of Green Gables keeps charming generation after generation of girls with its account of the romance of life for a young girl in Prince Edward Island. Young Japanese women continue to come to PEI to get married or to visit the house where Anne was supposed to have lived. Today there are many excellent books with female characters that girls will find appealing. This web shows some of the directions that this interest field can take.

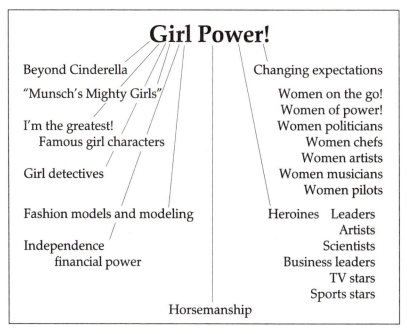

## Beyond Cinderella

One positive development in the last few years has been the emergence of strong girl characters in children's literature to act as role models. Educators need to do everything they can to remove the negative stereotypes of women and provide positive imaging. The following books are examples of ones with strong female characters that girls might enjoy:

Ainsworth, Ken. *Building a Solitaire Game and a Peg Board* (Building Together Series). A dad helps his daughter to safely build a game board. See also: *Building A Shelf and a Bike Rack.*

Branford, Henrietta. *Dimanche Diller.* Orphaned in Greece when her parent's luxury yacht sank in a storm, Dimanche is a survivor. She outwits a tough old woman who masquerades as a nun and tries to kill her to get her big inheritance.

Brewster, Hugh. *Anastasia's Album: The Last Tsar's Youngest Daughter Tells Her Own Story.* A tale of mystery and intrigue told with photographs of the family life and last days of the family of Tsar Nicholas II.

Calmenson, Stephanie and Joanna Cole. *The Gator Girls: Rockin' Reptiles* (Beech Tree Chapter Books). A new gator in town upsets Allie and Amy's friendship.

Cleary, Beverly. *Muggie Maggie.* In grade three, Maggie resolves never to learn how to write cursive, never!

Cleary, Beverly. *Ramona and Her Father.* Dad loses his job and our heroine tries to help out, even to get him to stop smoking.

Conrad, Pan. *Staying Nine* (A Trophy Chapter Book). Heather thinks that nine is just the perfect age—why get older?

Danziger, Paula. *Amber Brown is Not a Crayon.* When her friend moves away, Amber is faced with not having a best friend.

Enderle, Judith and Stephanie Tessler. *What's the Matter, Kelly Beans?* What a family—everybody is wonderful and does wonderful things—all except eight-year-old Kelly!

Henkes, Kevin. *Lily's Purple Plastic Purse.* When her new purse gets her into trouble at school, Lily changes her mind about her best teacher.

Karr, Kathleen. *The Lighthouse Mermaid* (Hyperion Chapters). During a storm, Kate has to help in the rescue—could it really be a mermaid?

Lasky, Kathryn. *Grace the Pirate* (Hyperion Chapters). A girl wants to show her pirate father Black Oak O'Malley that she can sail too.

Little, Jean. *From Anna.* A young immigrant girl has trouble adjusting because of her eyesight problems.

Lowell, Melissa. *Silver Blades on the Edge* (Gold Medal Dreams, #1). Tori knows she is ill but keeps going to compete in the national figure skating championships anyway.

Lowry, Lois. *Anastasia Absolutely.* Oops! She put a package of dog feces in the mailbox instead of her mother's letter. Is this a federal offence?

Lowry, Lois. *Anastasia, Ask Your Analyst.* To cope with her embarrassing family and three-year-old genius brother, Anastasia is convinced she is disturbed and needs an analyst.

Lowry, Lois. *Anastasia Krupnik.* A with-it girl who loves to keeps lists of the things she loves and hates.

Naylor, Phyllis Reynolds. *Agony of Alice.* What a mistake-filled life she is having. Will she ever survive grade six?

Wyatt, Valerie. *The Science Book for Girls and Other Intelligent Beings.* Go for it! Everyday science activities with a be-a-scientist approach, along with visual puzzles and mind benders.

### KidLink: I'm the Greatest!

Invite students to nominate girl characters they think should be considered the greatest. These will likely be characters that have strength of their values and beliefs, determination to get out and do things and a zest for life. Naturally, they will have to support their suggestions with reasons. Some of the nominees might include: Anastasia Krupnik;

Ramona; Alice; Dimanche Diller; Lily (of "Purple Purse" fame); Harriet the Spy; Amber Brown.

Kids may wish to assume the character of one of the girls and be interviewed on mock television shows about life, interests and hobbies. Make "I'm the Greatest!" promotion name tags or a display on a bulletin board. By all means have a mock election, encouraging supporters of each girl to address the class and tell why she should win the "I'm the Greatest!" award.

The nominees for this year will surely be supported by many others, including: Anne from *Anne of Green Gables*, Heidi from *Heidi*, Lucy from the Narnia series, Leslie from *Bridge to Terabithia*, Jo from *Little Women*, Nancy Drew from her series, Sheila from *Sheila the Great*, Amelia Bedelia from her series, Meg from *Wrinkle in Time* and Laura Ingalls from *The Little House on the Prairie*. The world of folk tales could offer support too, especially from such characters as Cinderella, Snow White, Beauty (and the beast), Mulan, Rapunzel, Rose Red and maybe Tinkerbell.

### AuthorLink: Munsch's Mighty Girls

Canada's Robert Munsch has created many kid-proven picture books. Older readers need to somehow be given permission to return to these books and enjoy them. Ask readers to reread the books to see if they can find the keys to his success. Obviously, they are full of wit, sound and noise expressions, and a sense of the impossible actions all kids wish they could do.

But the secret in all Munsch's books is that in the end, the kids get the power! And in many of his books, it is the girls who get the power! A few where this is the case include: *From Far Away; Moira's Birthday; The Paper Bag Princess; Pigs; Stephanie's Ponytail*.

### AuthorLink: Karen Cushman

"I want to go back to a time when knights were knights and girls had a romantic life."

Forget it! Get real!

Karen Cushman is a medievalist who has taught the subject at the university level. She is fascinated by what life was really like for young girls during that time. In *Catherine, Called Birdy*, she shares, in diary form, what daily life was like for the daughter of a local baron. Birdy, who feels she is trapped like a bird in a cage, is told exactly what her role as a woman will be, but she has other ideas, especially when it comes to who will be her husband—certainly not the dreadful older man her father has suggested.

In *The Midwife's Apprentice*, Dung Beetle was living in a dung heap to keep warm until the local midwife took her on as an assistant. After being mistaken for a woman named Alyce, she adopts the name for herself, and her life changes dramatically.

**Girls Make Better Detectives**

It is interesting to note how many girls are successful detectives in novels. We only have to think of the popular Nancy Drew. It could be argued that many of the boy and girl detective teams really rely on the intuition and brains of the girl to solve the case ...

*KidLink: Prove It!*

Challenge your reluctant readers to find examples that prove whether girls really do make better detectives. This activity is more fun and more appealing if done in teams. Groups of kids can read books in the same series and talk about what they discover. A great debate could be held with two different teams discussing whether they agree or not. Are girls better detectives? If so, how and why? Read some of these suggested titles to find out:

Adler, David. *Cam Jansen and the Mystery of Flight 54* (A Cam Jansen Adventure). While at the airport to meet their aunt, Cam's quick thinking solves the case of the missing French girl.

Bailey, Linda. *How Come the Best Clues Are Always in the Garbage?* (A Stevie Diamond Mystery). Eleven-year-old Stevie has a job to do—she has to catch a robber. See also: *How Can I Be a Detective If I Have to Baby-Sit?*

Blyton, Enid. *Castle of Adventure* (Adventure Series). Why were the locals afraid of this castle?

Conford, Ellen. *A Case for Jenny Archer*. After reading detective books, Jenny becomes suspicious of the neighbors. Are they just fixing up the house or are they a gang of criminals?

Heneghan, Jim. *The Trail of the Chocolate Thief*. Mystery buffs will follow Clarice, Sadie and Brick as they try to solve what is happening in their neighborhood.

Saunders, Susan. *The Revenge of the Pirate Ghost* (A Trophy Chapter Book: The Black Cat Club). Check out the ghost who ate chocolate and the curse of the cat mummy.

Warner, Gertrude Chandler. *The Firehouse Mystery* (The Box Car Children, #56). Popular quartet of kids who used to live with their grandmother, but now live in a firehouse or wherever the mystery dictates.

Weir, Joan. *Sky Lodge Mystery and Other Stories* (Mystery Club). A school's mystery club sets out to get involved. Could they do better if one of them was a girl?

Wilson, Eric. *Ghost of Lunenburg Manor*. Liz Austen works with her brother Tom to solve mysteries set all across Canada—especially in a so-called haunted house in Nova Scotia.

A few self-help detective manuals that are worth a look include:

Civardi, Anne, et al. *The Usborne Detective's Handbook*. A fully illustrated guide to becoming a better detective; packed with strategies, skill improvement and amusing suggestions.

Coleman, Michael. *Internet Detectives: Speed Surf*. A mysterious message appears on the computer screen and the trio of Josh, Rob and Tomsyn feel it's a secret code—something they must decode to find the art thief.

Schwartz, Alvin. *The Cat's Elbow and Other Secret Languages*. Can you speak Pig Latin, Medical Greek, King Tut, Thief Talk or the Cat's Elbow?

## KidLink: *My Journal*

The appeal of keeping a journal is strong for many readers, especially for those who want to become detectives, but not for reluctant readers as they are often reluctant writers too. Recently, however, several publishers have begun to market very appealing journal-type books. Gone are the blank pages and in are zippy comments, humor and categories to complete. Try these:

Kranz, Linda. *All About ME: A Keepsake Journal for Kids*. Purple text on the sides and watercolor illustrations give ideas of what to write.

Moss, Marissa. *My Notebook (with help from Amelia) by ___ and Marissa Moss*. With the free purple pen, kids can respond to the suggestions hand-printed by Amelia (we guess) on the edges and top of the page. This notebook follows *Amelia's Notebook*, which is Amelia's actual journal, complete with her felt pen drawings of herself and girlfriends. There is lots of space to write.

**Horses, Horses, Horses!**

Many girls simply love horses! If they are fortunate, they might even have a horse of their own; if not, they may have dreams of someday owning one. A lot of youngsters go for riding lessons at local stables and are interested in everything about horses: types, care, equipment, food and training. Titles to keep young equestrians contented include:

Betancourt, Jeanne. *The Missing Pony Pal* (Pony Pals). Just because she and Snow White had a fall, will Lulu quit riding?

Bryant, Bonnie. *English Horse* (The Saddle Club, #79). The British riders are coming to compete. Will they win?

Budd, Jackie. *Horses*. A highly visual look at horse history, behavior, breeding, riding and jumping. Features a fold-out diagram of a stable.

Campbell, Joanna. *Stirling's Second Chance* (Thoroughbred Series, #26). Everyone wonders if Christina and Sterling have what it takes to win.

Edwards, Elwyn Hartley. *Horse: A Visual Guide to Over 100 Horse Breeds from around the World* (Eyewitness Handbook). A thorough look at individual breeds with characteristics noted.

Everts, Tammy and Bobbie Kalman. *Horses*. If you want to be a rider, you need to know a lot about horses: kinds, parts, markings, gaits and how to care for them.

Pritchard, Louise. *My Pony*. Outstanding organization of material by relevant topics, with multiple step-by-step diagrams, as well as an abundance of photos focusing on small details such as types of food, poisonous plants and items in a grooming kit.

Shub, Elizabeth. *The White Stallion* (A Bantam First Skylark). A historical tale set in 1845 of a young girl, Gretchen, who got lost from her wagon train and was saved by a mysterious white horse.

## KidLink: Horse Terms

Learning to read implies a great deal of word recognition or vocabulary development. One thing we can say with certainty is that the horse set has a good many "in" terms that riders and enthusiasts use in their daily conversations. To learn these words is no difficulty for reluctant readers, as their interest overcomes any preconceived notion of difficulty. These are the words they hear around the stables and the words they will easily learn to recognize so that they can be "in" with their crowd. Teachers and parents have to learn this vocabulary in order to be able to use the terms correctly.

We have included a list of such words below so that they can be linked to class events. Why not use the "word of the day" idea to hunt down their history and find out how they are used? Decide with the kids how these words will be shared with others, for example, in a bulletin board display or in a story.

---

### HORSES, HORSES, HORSES

| Colors: | Stable Terms: |
|---|---|
| Bay | Manger |
| Chestnut | Pitchfork |
| Dappled gray | Shavings |
| Gray, white | Wheelbarrow |
| Buckskin | Buckets |
| Piebald | Salt block |
| Pinto | Watering trough |
| Black | Barn broom |
| Fleabitten gray | Hay net |
| Appaloosa | Box stall |
| Palomino | Tie stall |
| Dunn | Scoop |

| Horse Types: | Grooming Kit: |
|---|---|
| Hunter | Body brush |
| Jumper | Dandy brush |
| Polo | Hoof pick |
| Cattle pony | Curry comb |
| Cow horse/pony | Mane comb |
| Hack | |
| Hunter back | Tack: |
| Show pony | Saddle |
| Carriage horse/pony | Pommel |
| "Walk/trot" pony | Breast plate |
| "Backyard" pony | Stirrups |
| Race horse | Girth |
| Thoroughbred | |

## KidLink: Famous Horses

When it comes to horses, several famous ones come to mind: Black Beauty, the Black Stallion, King of the Wind, Man O'War, Misty of Chincoteaque and My Friend Flicka. These are the classic ones found in novels. Ask the kids to collect the names of equally famous horses taken from real life, and together with fictional horses, create a bulletin board or a photo album with information and drawings.

## Laughs!

We all need to laugh! Kids who are reluctant readers commonly face a life that is very serious indeed. They are "so into failure" that they see everything that happens to them as increasing their failure. Consequently, anytime they can laugh at the world and at themselves lightens their load and allows them to relax enough to attend to reading instead of worrying about not reading.

There is a clown in every one of us! If children experience failure and get laughed at in a classroom, they often resort to becoming the class clown—acting silly when serious answers are expected. Such clowning is often a cover-up for reading and writing troubles. Lack of comprehension often results in a joking, inattentive student. There are many subtleties of clowning around, yet each represents the only way these kids see to get people to like them.

While a reluctant reader as class clown may seem inappropriate, we ourselves must remember that we sometimes act like clowns because it allows for a feeling of spontaneity, happiness, joy, acceptance and "being okay." It gives us a sense of release and a sense of freedom. It also hides other feelings we might have of insecurity, loneliness and inferiority. It gives us a mask to hide behind—to allow the positive or negative forces in our lives to take over. So too for reluctant readers.

Clowns do make a difference in our lives; why else are there hospital clowns to cheer up the patients? This is one of the exciting developments in children's hospitals, as clowns allow healing laughter to be released. Kids are spontaneous and will react to a clown, much like they do to a doll or puppet. They enter into the fantasy of it. Canadian writer Camilla Gryski is a clown at Toronto's Hospital for Sick Children. No doubt she uses her string games to entice youngsters out of their dark moments. These games can be found in her books: *Cat's Cradle, Owl's Eyes: A Book of String Games; Many Stars and More String Games;* and *Super String Games.*

We do need to laugh, perhaps at this very moment. Why not check the Web out for a chuckle? Try *www.laffsforkids.com* or *www.bconney.net/~kidworld/* for a start.

We all need to laugh and it's easy: remember that we use fewer muscles to smile than to frown! What we laugh at is a matter of personal taste and experience. Sometimes kids need to discuss what is funny, especially when it is not basic slapstick, hit-em-roll-em humor. Double meanings, wit and colorful expression may be missed if not shared in advance. The web below shows just a few of the possible topics within this interest field.

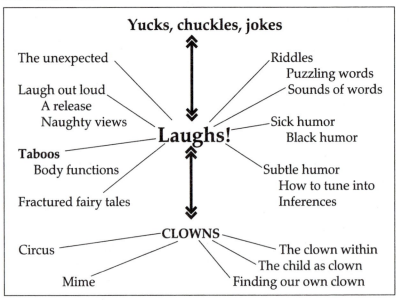

## Laugh and Read

Claire Mackay's *Laughs*, a hilarious collection of funny stories, is a splendid way to commence a laughable approach to reading. Also refer to chapter four's word-play section for other references. To get a chuckle try these too:

Browne, Anthony. *Willy the Wimp*. A puny kid gorilla trains to become a "he" man in an attempt to overcome the neighborhood bullies and impress his girlfriend Millie.

Fleischman, Sid. *McBroom's Wonderful One-Acre Farm* (Beech Tree Chapter Books). Three hilarious tall tales.

Jennings, Paul. *The Cabbage Patch War*. A neighborhood dispute turns into a war!

Kawakami, Kenji. Translated from the Japanese by Dan Paia. *99 More Unuseless Japanese Inventions: The Art of Chindogu*. Hilarious inventions that did not quite make it; battery operated rotating spaghetti fork, diet dishes cut in half by a mirror or shirtless sleeves.

King-Smith, Dick. *Babe: The Gallant Pig*. Adopted by a sheepdog, this runt becomes an award winning sheep-pig!

McMullan, K.H. *The New Kid at School* (Dragon Slayers' Academy). Hilarious account of a young boy studying at knight school.

McNaughton, Colin. *Here Come the Aliens!* The fleet of space ships arrive and so do the aliens in every shape, size, color and contortion! Hide! Rollicking text with repetition, rhyme and rhythm.

Mowat, Farley. *Owls in the Family*. Trying to help injured owls can cause unexpected results.

Park, Barbara. *June B. Jones and Some Sneaky Peeky Spring* (A First Stepping Stone Book). One of the funniest kindergartners is a great "spy" because she has sneaky feet.

Pilkey, Dav. *The Silly Gooses*. Six short hilarious chapters about the antics of silly Mr. Goose.

Pinkwater, Daniel. *Mush: A Dog from Space*. Although her parents object to a dog, when Kelly meets Mush, a talking mushamute from planet Growl-Woof-Woof, all havoc breaks out in this nonsensical fantasy.

Robinson, Barbara. *The Best Christmas Pageant Ever*. When the Herdman kids arrive—lying, stealing and smoking cigars—a totally new image is given to the annual pageant.

Yep, Laurence. *Later, Gator*. It seemed like a good idea to give an alligator as a birthday present to his brother. Turtles are boring!

## AuthorLink: "Clearly Cleary"

Stop being such a pest! Many younger parents and teachers will be able to recall episodes of Ramona or Henry Huggins that they enjoyed as a child. We laughed then and we laugh now. Beverly Cleary's vivid recall of childhood experiences has a timeless quality and appeals to many generations of readers. Granted, some have become dated, but many remain, including such poignant issues so important to youngsters as: their dad trying to stop smoking, the new baby arriving, as well as fair and equal treatment with siblings. Her writing style, although that of a talented wordsmith, is deceptively easy for readers, a great plus for reluctant readers. In *Socks,* we see the modern North American nuclear family—husband, wife and cat—being upset by the arrival of a horrible beast—the new baby! Kids who are in the same position will empathize with the cat, Socks.

Prepare to laugh and to understand life just a bit better as you read the following Cleary titles: *Dear Mr. Henshaw; The Mouse and the Motorcycle; Ramona and her Father; Ramona the Pest; Socks.*

## Taboos

Oh, to be naughty and still nice! Kids love to chuckle over the taboos of society—to push the edges but not get in trouble. Books about taboos allow reluctant readers another avenue for not being rigidly correct all the time and help them to adopt a more flexible attitude. The television show *South Park* is a prime example of daring to go too far. The characters say what kids and even adults wouldn't dream of saying in public.

Part of the success of Robert Munsch's picture books, particularly *The Paperbag Princess, David's Father, Moira's Birthday* and *Pigs* is that in them it is the kids who have the real power and who do hilarious taboo actions.

One of the most popular "taboo" titles, with over one million copies sold, is Dav Pilkey's "epic novel," *The Adventures of Captain Underpants.* Polite people don't talk about underpants, and to see a cartoon man in them on the cover is hysterically funny for kids. In this book, two kids in trouble with the school principal are called into his office for creating their own comic, "The Adventures of Captain Underpants," a fighter of crime. They succeed in hypnotizing him and convincing him that he is indeed Captain Underpants. After stripping down to his !!!, off he goes to face a set of robbers. Pilkey's expressive cartoons, his play with text sizes and shapes, and his off-the-wall humor captivate reluctant readers. Adults too! Here are a few other taboo titles to try:

Holzwarth, Werner. *The Story of the Little Mole Who Knew It Was None of His Business.* When the young animal couldn't keep his nose out of things, he got into trouble.

Lattimore, Deborah Nourse. *I Wonder What's Under There? A Brief History of Underwear* (A Lift-the-Flap Book). Be brave, take a peek! The revealing story of petticoats and pre-jockey shorts.

Munsch, Robert. *Good Families Don't*. Ever see a fart? You may soon be plagued by one.

*Planet Dexter's Grossology: Gross Science That Kids Want to Learn!* (CD-ROM) —from the book by Sylvia Branzei. Science, rudely covering such things as zits, burps, snot, spit, smelly feet and a lot more!

Strasser, Todd. *Kids' Book of Gross Facts and Feats*. A browser's guide to yucky information.

Walker, S. *Heads and Tails* (A Lift-the-Flap Book). A "naughty" rear-view glimpse of animals. Lift the tail to confirm what it is!

## KidLink: Kids as Jokers

Many reluctant readers find the TV series *South Park* to be hilariously funny. Talk of a generation gap ... many adults find it is in poor taste, vulgar, racist, sexist, violent—an altogether negative experience. While we may not like the off-color humor, our need for humor and jokes is what justifies an entire comedy network. In class, or indeed at the dinner table, establish a joke time; a fast-paced time when anyone who has a joke, riddle or funny story can tell it. Try to make the atmosphere friendly and accepting, especially if the punch lines get forgotten! No sitting in rows in the classroom!

This activity will encourage reluctant readers to search for joke books. Here are a few good ones:

- Ahlberg, Janet and Allan. *The Ha Ha Bonk Book*.
- Berger, Melvin. *One Hundred and One Spooky Halloween Jokes*.
- Christopher, Matt. *Baseball Jokes and Riddles*.
- Eckstein, Joan and Joyce Gleit. *The Best Joke Book for Kids*.
- Hall, Cathy. *One Hundred One Cat and Dog Jokes*.
- Hall, Katy and Lisa Eisenberg. *Mummy Riddles*.
- Hall, Katy and Lisa Eisenberg. *Sheepish Riddles*.
- Perret, Gene. *Super Funny School Jokes*.
- Risinger, Matt and Phillip Yates. *Great Book of Zany Jokes*.
- Rothaus, Jim. *Baseball Jokes*.

## AuthorLink: Roald Dahl

Delightfully wicked humor!

Of all the great fantasies written for children, Roald Dahl's remain near the top of the list. *Charlie and the Chocolate Factory*, a clever, tongue-in-cheek, morality tale, and *James and the Giant Peach* are beloved by children of all ages. Dahl simply creates absurd situations that children think are funny. His quirky humor has created a gallery of memorable characters: some of whom are models of goodness, some completely zany, and others absolutely repulsive. He is able to portray the perspectives of all these different characters with gleeful precision.

Dahl has the knack of speaking directly to kids, even if adults don't agree. In all his writing, Dahl's wicked sense of humor comes through: kids mention the strange humor or that the book was funny in a sick way. Whatever one thinks of the story, kid readers are lost in their imaginations, far beyond the pages of the book. Films and videos featuring Charlie, James and Matilda help to increase the popularity of his work for reluctant readers. A few of Dahl's most popular titles include: *The BFG; Charlie and the Chocolate Factory; James and the Giant Peach; Matilda; The Witches.*

### Fractured Fairy Tales

Get kissed by a frog and .... Wait a minute, no frog is going to kiss me! Kids find fractured retellings of folk tales to be hilarious. They will laugh and joke about the stories, and of course have a great time devising their own versions. Little do they realize that they are getting all the basic elements of folklore in their changed versions. Remember, it all started with a kiss, or was it a huff and a puff, Mr. Wolf? Some excellent titles include:

Auch, Mary Jane. *Peeping Beauty.* No doubt Aesop would approve; a hen who wants to be a famous ballerina outwits a hungry fox.

Brown, Ruth. *The World That Jack Built.* An ecological version of what happens to the house (world) that Jack (we) build(s).

French, Fiona. *Snow White in New York.* What a change a roaring '20s setting makes to this traditional story.

Jackson, Ellen. *Cinder Edna.* Cinderella had a friend, Edna, and the prince had a brother—put them together and ... happily ever after. A saucy tale.

Ketteman, Helen. *Buba the Cowboy Prince: A Fractured Texas Tale.* Rollickin' brand of western humor in which a lonely cowhand is bossed around by a wicked stepfather and nasty stepbrothers. Thank goodness rancher Ms. Lureen is out to find herself a real man!

Little, Jean and Maggie de Vries. *Once Upon a Golden Apple.* Dad starts to read a tale but gets it wrong and his two kids loudly correct him, "No, No, NO!" They know better! What fun!

Lobel, Arnold. *Fables.* Fables about the "crocodile in the bedroom" and 19 other animals in uncanny situations.

Munsch, Robert. *The Paper Bag Princess.* One of the first fractured tales to come out—this princess isn't going to stand for the snooty behavior of an ordinary prince!

Napoli, Donna Jo. *The Prince of the Pond.* A peculiar new frog astounds the local pond dwellers. He gets his feet tangled up when jumping, won't eat bugs and calls himself "De Fawg Pin."

Palatini, Margie. *Piggie Pie.* A witch doesn't get any pigs for her pie, but then, the wolf didn't either!

Perlman, Janet. *Cinderella Penguin or The Little Glass Flipper*. A poorly treated penguin rises to fame and fortune after the prince finds her glass flipper.

Scieszka, Jon. *Squids Will Be Squids: Fresh Morals, Beastly Fables*. Wild illustrations highlight outrageous fables with their sassy morals.

Scieszka, Jon. *The Frog Prince*. ... and the prince and the princess lived happily ever after in their castle away from the pond—forget it!

Scieszka, Jon. *The True Story of the Three Little Pigs by A. Wolf*. Feeling framed, a wolf confesses the truth from his perspective.

## ⚭ *KidLink: This Will Crack You Up!*

Of course, after reading one of these hilarious fractured tales, kids will want to retell a story of their own. In fact, why not have them place it in your own community? Then the local color of places and people can be added to enhance the telling. Naturally, the kids should be encouraged to tell (or read!) their stories to younger kids.

## Survival!

One of the traditional themes of Canadian literature for adults and children is survival. Obviously this relates frequently to the harshness of winter, with its storms and frigid temperatures—where the wind chill becomes a major factor in daily survival. If you've never been caught in a complete whiteout while driving on a remote road, you simply cannot comprehend the danger of a blizzard, nor the fear of being caught in one.

Survival stories are not exclusively set in an outdoor wilderness setting though. The wilderness can also be an urban setting, fantasy world, futuristic landscape, past place or even within ourselves. Survival is necessary in a lot of unusual situations. Consider Max, who went to "Where the Wild Things Are" and returned! One of our great survivalists! Use the web on the following page as a starting place for connecting to a variety of survival topics.

### Survival in the Wilderness

All kids are fascinated by survival stories, especially those set in the wilderness. Why? Perhaps it is the romance of the wild, the challenge of pitting oneself against the elements of nature, or just a vicarious escape from one's present situation.

How do survival stories come about? Sometimes it is a well-planned trip gone wrong, as in *Lost in the Barrens*; an accident such as a plane crash, as in *Hatchet*; or a personal escape to the wild, as in *Hunter in the Dark* and *Crabbe*.

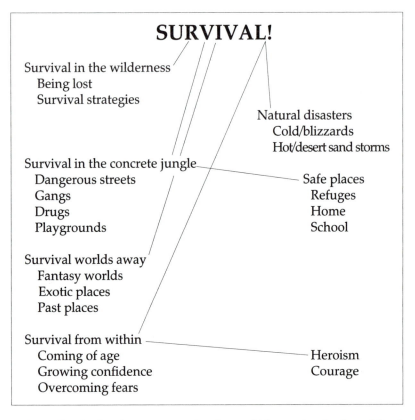

# SURVIVAL!

Survival in the wilderness
  Being lost
  Survival strategies

Natural disasters
Cold/blizzards
Hot/desert sand storms

Survival in the concrete jungle
  Dangerous streets
  Gangs
  Drugs
  Playgrounds

Safe places
Refuges
Home
School

Survival worlds away
  Fantasy worlds
  Exotic places
  Past places

Survival from within
  Coming of age
  Growing confidence
  Overcoming fears

Heroism
Courage

Basically, high adventure is what keeps kids coming back and back for more. Experience these titles and you'll see why.

Bell, William. *Crabbe.* An alcoholic teenager take the family canoe and heads to the wild to live for a year.

George, Jean Craighead. *Julie of the Wolves.* Caught in the barrens, a teenage girl must learn the ways of a wolf pack in order to survive.

George, Jean Craighead. *My Side of the Mountain.* A long lasting favorite! A boy runs away to live in a large tree for a year.

Hobbs, Will. *Beardance.* Would you give your life to save two grizzly bear cubs?

Houston, James. *Frozen Fire.* Two boys, one from an Inuit community and one from Toronto, are caught in a blizzard and need the skills of both cultures to escape alive.

Hughes, Monica. *Hunter in the Dark.* Fighting leukemia, a teenage boy borrows the family's truck and heads out to the wilderness to shoot a buck.

Mowat, Farley. *Lost in the Barrens.* Two boys, one from southern Canada and one from a First Nations community, get lost on a canoe trip in the North West Territories.

Sperry, Armstrong. *Call It Courage*. Afraid of the sea, Mafatu, the son of a Polynesian chief, sets out to prove his bravery.

### ⑩ *KidLink: What? Me Get Lost? I Can Survive!*

Many school districts have outdoor schools or centres—a wonderful part of their outdoor education program. If kids do not have access to such an experience, parents and teachers should certainly make an effort to educate them in survival techniques.

Encourage the kids to plan for a hike, an overnight one if possible. They will need to decide what they need to take with them for the trip (e.g. food, first aid equipment, clothing, directional aids, reading material, etc.). This type of planning involves active list making. Invite a member of a hiking club or a park warden to come to talk about hiking safety. This person could share strategies of what to do if you should get lost ... hug a tree? Make certain to share *My Side of the Mountain*, *Hatchet* and *Crabbe*; making lists of the techniques used by the characters to survive.

Why not do a special focus on an outdoor activity such as rock climbing? Bring into the classroom the latest magazines such as *Climber*, *High Mountain Sports* and *Climbing*. The photographs are wonderful. The group could do small climbs in the community as a way of starting activities that could be done with their parents! The kids may not be able to really do it, but may still like to read about it.

### ⑩ *AuthorLink: Gary Paulsen*

Want to get lost in an adventure?

Based on his Minnesota fur trapping days, many of Paulsen's books exude the romance of a wilderness adventure, yet there is always a respect for the ways of nature, the living creatures in the wilderness and an ever-present realization of the importance of personal survival. As many of his novels relate to personal experience, they place real characters in real settings, facing real problems. This contemporary realism frequently pits the individual against the wild in a quest for survival. Paulsen's writing style is direct, concisely integrating description important to the action and forever pushing the story to its conclusion. Could it be that Paulsen's passion for reading as a child enriches the storytelling quality in his books? Once snared, reluctant readers will read until they finish his books.

This prolific writer is a favourite with reluctant readers. Probably the best way to get them going is to share *Hatchet* with them. What would it be like to be flying in a small airplane in which the pilot has a heart attack and dies? How would you survive? What if you landed in the wilderness and couldn't summon help?

Several of his titles are available in audiocassette format, thus enhancing their appeal. Give these titles a try: *Brian's Winter; Dogsong; Hatchet; My Life in Dog Years.*

### Survival in the Concrete Jungle

Don't fool yourself.

There's danger at each turning point.

Many city streets are simply not safe to walk anymore, especially after sunset. In some large cities, fear runs rampant in the inner city.

The question remains, "How does a kid survive?" It is obviously through a combination of knowledge, street smarts and an objective outlook on life. Some kids are on the streets by choice: the runaways of society, perhaps escaping for their lives or in search of love. A few may have been thrown out or cast aside by their dysfunctional families.

Often novels set in the concrete jungle provide a great deal of insight into the urban environment and into the lives of those who inhabit it. Despite the harshness of this environment, the stories are often rich in language and sensitivity, and nearly always conclude with an element of hope. Learn your street smarts by reading the following:

Bunting, Eve. *Fly Away Home.* What is it like to be a homeless dad and son at a major airport? A sparrow gives the boy hope for the future.

Bunting, Eve. *Smoky Night.* A frightening view of riots in Los Angeles by a young boy worried about his cat.

Bunting, Eve. *Your Move.* They may be painting graffiti, but when they get caught by "the Snakes," they run! James and his little brother have had enough. No gangs for them!

Fox, Paula. *Monkey Island.* A young boy's mother leaves him destitute on the streets. Luckily some homeless people look after him.

Gleitzman, Morris. *Blabber Mouth.* Unable to talk because of a birth defect, Rowena has difficulty in a new school.

Holman, Felice. *Slake's Limbo.* He lives in a subway until he becomes ill and when he is noticed, help arrives.

### ⦾ KidLink: I'm Street-Proofed!

"Look at me; I know the ways of the street! " Kids today need to be made aware of the dangers of the city, but also to be realistic about it and to know where to go to get help if needed. The importance of non-verbal behavior can be emphasized by using mime in the classroom. For example, how one walks tells a lot about us. Have the kids try choosing book characters and showing how they would walk. How you talk also indicates your confidence and awareness level. What do you say? Why not let the book characters try first!

There may be dangers and concerns in a city, but there are also many special safe places that only a few people know about. They are the secret places, the quiet lanes, the "one of a kind" views or the "only I know about these" places.

Ask the kids to talk about where a favorite book character might have a place they would share with only special people. Encourage reluctant readers to describe it.

Special places? Have you ever given a "smell" tour of your city? A "color" tour? A "tree" tour? A "sign" tour? A "mural" tour? We—kids, parents and teachers—often do not fully realize all the interesting places that exist in our own communities until we go out and discover them. When we do this, we gain a new interest in and perspective of the world.

## Survival Worlds Away

Beyond the light of the sun may exist galaxies and planets with other intelligent beings. They too may be in a survival mode, and it is evident that many novels relate to this theme. Other worlds also play an important part in the world of imagination—the land of fantasy. While J.R.R. Tolkien's *The Hobbit*, Richard Adams's *Watership Down* and Brian Jacques's *Redwall* series are enticing reads for many kids, they may prove to be too much of a challenge for reluctant readers. Use a video version or encourage them to put these books aside until they are older and able to read them.

Other classic examples of extraordinary worlds are in Lewis Carroll's *Alice in Wonderland*, Frank L. Baum's *The Wizard of Oz* and Mary Norton's *The Borrowers*. Each, quite different in tone, has evolved a unique world. Historical fiction gives us a glimpse of medieval times in Karen Cushman's *Catherine, Called Birdy* and World War Two in Lois Lowry's *Number the Stars*, Uri Orlev's *The Island on Bird Street* or Kit Pearson's *The Sky is Falling*. Time travel offers a way to get into the past as evidenced in Janet Lunn's *The Root Cellar*, Natalie Babbitt's *Tuck Everlasting* or Jane Yolen's *The Devil's Arithmetic*. Here are a few more titles worth exploring:

Hughes, Monica. *Keeper of the Isis Light*. A young girl has been adapted by her guardian so that she can live on a far flung planet.
Hughes, Monica. *The Golden Aquarians*. In 2092 Walt joins his engineer father on the planet Aqua where there is a project to terraform the environment.
L'Engle, Madeleine. *A Wrinkle in Time*. Imagine being able to "tesseract" to get to a place before you left!

Lewis, C.S. *The Lion, the Witch and the Wardrobe*. Once entered through the wardrobe, readers come into the mysteriously frozen land of Narnia. Challenging to read at many levels.

### KidLink: My World!

I've got a "world!"

Just as the kids did in C. S. Lewis's *The Lion, the Witch and the Wardrobe*, reluctant readers can be stimulated to create a new world in which to set a story. This simply must be done in groups as there is so much to talk about. Where would it be? Who would live there? How would they travel? What would they eat? What is its name? Does it have a crest? A flag? What is the major problem facing this world? Who might be able to help out?

## Survival from Within

We all go through trying times in our lives. It is amazing how some kids actually survive the awful situations in which they find themselves, which might include being victims of beatings, verbal or sexual abuse, and/or drugs or alcohol. Often, as members of dysfunctional families, they, or others, realize that they have to get out to survive. Several novels about foster parents, such as *The Great Gilly Hopkins*, *Pinballs* and *Adam and Eve and Pinch Me*, relate the experiences of kids being emotionally tough enough to survive. Sometimes survival is also a physical one, as in overcoming or accepting a disease such as cancer.

Kids sometimes choose to escape their problems in a negative way: by running away, by rebellious antisocial behavior or by retreating into a world of depression, alcohol or drugs. All the books written about this situation have a strong theme relating to our need to love and be loved. We simply cannot avoid it.

Kids who survive pull themselves up by their own boot straps and take responsibility for their actions. They end up stronger, more aware of the world and the people around them, and are perhaps even more sensitive to others. Finding inner strength, the coward can turn into a hero and the bully into a caring individual. You, too, may be changed if you read some of these:

Byars, Betsy. *Pinballs*. Three kids, all lonely and alienated, are placed in the same foster home—with touching and amusing results.
Cushman, Karen. *The Midwife's Apprentice*. Living in a dung heap, the main character learns about life and gains much self confidence.
Fox, Paula. *The Eagle Kite*. Liam's dad has AIDs and on this Thanksgiving he wants to be with him.
Johnston, Julie. *Adam and Eve and Pinch Me*. An unruly teen comes to the end of

foster homes when she arrives on a farm. Luckily, she has a notebook computer and records her reactions as she waits for her mother to come for her.

Little, Jean. *From Anna.* A young immigrant girl has trouble adjusting because of her eyesight problems.

Paterson, Katherine. *The Great Gilly Hopkins.* Rebellious Gilly, bright and hostile, doesn't know what she is to face in her new foster home—the unstinting love of Maxime Trotter.

Robinson, Barbara. *The Best Christmas Pageant Ever.* When the Herdman kids arrive—lying, stealing and smoking cigars—a totally new image is given to the annual pageant.

Wisniewski, David. *The Secret Knowledge of Grownups.* A hilarious revelation of a set of rules that adults put onto kids, but with the truth behind it!

## *KidLink: I'm Thumbody!*

Reluctant readers are kids who need to be reminded of all the good things about themselves. Come to think of it, we all need to do this at times.

For this strategy all you need to do is to bring a stamp pad into the classroom and let each kid put their thumb into it, and then onto a piece of paper. Voilà! A thumbprint. We have immediately slipped into the world of fingerprinting.

Make posters saying "I'm Thumbody!" Ask the students to make lists of positive traits of people, including themselves. Enlarge them on the photocopy machine.

Fingerprints? Invite police officers in to talk about how they do the process and how fingerprints differ from each other.

Fingerprint art? You bet—animals and people. Why, creative reluctant readers could even make cartoons from our "thumbodies!"

## Claws!

If there is one thing that reluctant readers are willing to share, it is information and stories about their pets—especially their cats and dogs. Thus, encouraged to talk, kids soon reveal the value of having pets: shared love, friendship, acceptance, patience and the ease of being with a stuffed or imaginary cat or dog! All kids want pets that are special and give them the attention and envy of their peer group. Such things as parrots, iguanas, boa constrictors and fighting fish will do—but oh, how wonderful it would be to have a "small" dinosaur! Check out the web on the following page to see just a few of the many topics within this interest field.

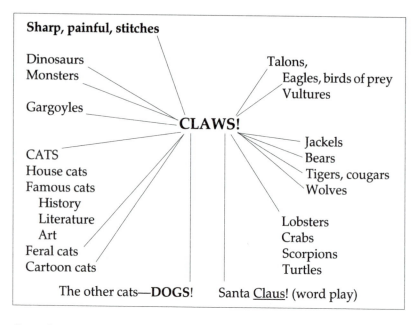

**Sharp, painful, stitches**

Dinosaurs
Monsters

Gargoyles

**CLAWS!**

CATS
House cats
Famous cats
   History
    Literature
    Art
Feral cats
Cartoon cats

The other cats—**DOGS!**

Talons,
  Eagles, birds of prey
  Vultures

Jackels
Bears
Tigers, cougars
Wolves

Lobsters
Crabs
Scorpions
Turtles

Santa <u>Claus</u>! (word play)

**Cats, Cats, Cats!**

It is soon obvious that cat lovers are passionate about their pets. Could it be because cats are such mysterious animals: very intelligent and exceptionally independent? Much of the writing that is done in school refers to the antics of kids' cats, and frequently when a cat dies it is has the same impact as a human being's passing. One thing that is often noted with reluctant readers is that they are passionate about their pets—especially if they have a cat.

Nicola Bayley's *The Necessary Cat* is a "celebration of cats in picture and word." A great sense of attachment is felt through the wit and humor evident in this rather eclectic assortment. The book is a browser's delight—each page is so different from the ones before.

We all know about Dr. Seuss's *Cat in the Hat*, but do you know about these other "catty" titles?

Arnold, Caroline. *Cats in from the Wild*. Answers questions about house cat behavior by looking at that of wildcats.
Bryan, Ashley. *The Cat's Purr*. A folk tale set in the Antilles.
Calhoun, Mary. *Cross-Country Cat*. Accidentally left behind in a ski lodge, Henry, a hero of a cat, chooses to save himself. The first adventure of many: *Hot-Air Henry*, *Henry the Sailor Cat*, and *High-Wire Henry*.
Cleary, Beverly. *Socks*. When the new baby comes home, the cat has trouble figuring out if her family still loves her.

Clutton-Brock, Juliet. *Cat* (Eyewitness Book). A close up view of a host of cats and their behavior.

Evans, Mark. *Kitten: A Practical Guide to Caring for Your Kitten* (ASPCA Pet Care Guides For Kids). A visual introduction to providing TLC to your pet.

Fine, Anne. *The Diary of a Killer Cat*. First it's a dead bird, and then a mouse—what's next?

*Fun With Your Cat: A Science Kit*. Activities to check your cat's preference for color, taste and personality.

Hodge, Deborah. *Wild Cats: Cougars, Bobcats and Lynx*. Life facts about this trio of felines.

Larrick, Nancy, ed. *Cats are Cats: Poems*. A poetic glimpse of favorite cats from young to old.

Lauber, Patricia. *The True-or-False Book of Cats*. Take the test and see if you know what is right for your cat!

Lesynski, Loris. *Catmagic*. The ladies of the Witches' Retirement Home work a spell together to help their cat—or did he outsmart them?

Lovka, Bob. *The Splendid Little Book of All Things Cats*. All you need to know about your cat.

O'Neill, Amanda. *Cats*. A visual guide to your cat, along with information about cat evolution, history, breeds and behavior.

Priceman, Marjorie. *My Nine Lives by Clio*. Delight in this short version of a remarkable cat's diary, featuring its nine lives in nine centuries.

Wild, Margaret. *The Very Best of Friends*. The loving friendship between James and Jessie is changed when James dies, and the cat and Jessie have to learn to get on with each other. What a personality this cat has as it acts out its grief.

Young, Ed. *Cat and Rat: The Legend of the Chinese Zodiac*. When the Jade Emperor invited the animals to a race in order to be selected as zodiac signs, the cat was eager to run ... well, now you will know why cats hate rats so much.

### *KidLink: Cat Language in English*

The English language is just filled with wonderful "catty" words and expressions. Some of these include: scaredy cat, witches cat, cat's paw, wild cat, catcall, and cat-eyed. Encourage kids to collect them and illustrate them for a bulletin board. What fun they will have doing this.

Is catgut from a cat? Can cats' eyes in the dark actually glow? Have you heard of these expressions? Why not find out their meanings and illustrate them? Here are some more:

- A cat has nine lives;
- Cat and fiddle;
- Cat-o'-nine-tails;
- Cat's cradle;
- Cat's eye;
- Catacomb;
- It is raining cats and dogs;

- See how the cat jumps;
- Sick as a cat;
- The cat's pajamas;
- To bell the cat;
- To grin like a Cheshire cat;
- To let the cat out of the bag;
- To put the cat among the pigeons;
- When the cat's away the mice will play.

### KidLink: Famous Cats

Have kids collect references and photographs of cats that are famous in history, literature and art. We know that you can go well beyond *The Cat in the Hat!* Here are a few to get you started:

- Cheshire Cat;
- Dick Whittington's cat;
- Felix the Cat;
- Pooh's cat, Tigger;
- Mummified cats of Egypt;
- Macavity the Mystery Cat (T.S. Elliot).

### KidLink: Garfield and Company

Cartoons such as Garfield are a great source of reading pleasure and good to pattern after. There is very little to write and most of the meaning is in the pictures. Invite your reluctant readers to draw what they can't readily put into words.

### Dogs— The Other Cats!

Surprisingly, not everyone is a cat lover. Some people respect cats, some hate them, and others prefer dogs! For reluctant readers, one of the greatest things about dogs is that they like to play and can be very funny. There is more than enough seriousness in most reluctant readers' lives and some turn their particular humorous friend into their best listener. For others, having any pet, especially one as big as a dog, is an impossibility. The only experience they can have is the vicarious one we give them through books.

One of the most remarkable literary dog lovers is William Wegman, who uses his weimaranger dogs to portray humans in hilarious editions of *Cinderella, Little Red Riding Hood, Mother Goose* and *Farm Days*. He has even created an alphabet book with letters constructed by his dogs. The newest one is always definitely one you won't want to miss. Here are some other titles that have "gone to the dogs!"

Allen, Eleanor. *Ghost Dog.* Kim finds the dog of her dreams, only you can see through him!

Brett, Jan. *The First Dog.* How Paleowolf became a cave boy's companion.

Byars, Betsy. *Tornado* (A Trophy Chapter Book). While taking shelter from a tornado, a farm hand tells stories about his pet dog, Tornado.

Clark, Margaret and Phil Hayes. *Meatball's Good Dog Day.* Causing chaos was this dog's chief interest, and he does it uncannily well.

Evans, Mark. *Puppy* (ASPCA Pet Care Guides for Kids). Describes the care and feeding of your pet.

Gerstein, Mordicai. *The New Creatures.* Long ago when dogs and cats ruled the world ... maybe dogs aren't as dumb as they look!

Griffith, Helen W. *Foxy.* Camping in the Florida Keys, a family comes across a fox-like dog and tries to befriend it.

Hall, Lynn. *Barry the Saint Bernard.* Several tales of how a dog saved people on the snowy mountain slopes.

Ling, Mary. *Amazing Wolves, Dogs and Foxes* (Amazing Worlds). An information book on the lives of wolves and wild dogs: their heirarchy, communication and senses.

Little, Jean. *Different Dragons.* A boy, visiting his aunt, is terrified of a dog, only to find it's as fearful of lightning as he is.

Little, Jean. *Mine for Keeps.* A young girl with cerebral palsy gets no special privileges at home or at school, only from her dog.

Paulsen, Gary. *My Life in Dog Years.* Reminiscences of nine dogs in his life: their character and influence on him.

Robertus, Polly M. *The Dog Who Had Kittens.* Baxter, a sad bassett hound, takes on raising abandoned kittens and creates a new life for himself.

Steig, William. *Dominic.* Off to see the world, a feisty young dog has many dangerous adventures and finally comes to an enchanted garden where he magically awakens a beautiful dog.

Waterton, Betty. *The Lighthouse Dog.* When the lighthouse keeper goes to buy a dog, he gets a huge one, but in a storm it turns out to be a lifesaver.

Wegman, William. *My Town.* Hilarious look at a town through its "dogpeople": teachers, firemen, repair shop employees, construction workers, barbers and doctors. The place has gone to the dogs!

## Dinosaurs

Really into "big" claws? Try the dinosaurs! Kids almost innately relate to dinosaurs. Many are walking encyclopedias of the facts. Reluctant readers may not read the "ands," "buts" or "thuses" of the text, but can certainly read "Styracosaurus," "Triceratops," "Stegosaurus" and "Tyrannosaurus."

Why not encourage these youngsters to become resource people in the school, going to classes of younger children to share their knowledge? Also, ask the teacher librarian to send a note to them when a new "dino" book arrives in the school resource centre, reserving a copy for them to look at first. Parents could ask a bookstore to notify them when a new dino title arrives. Some of the series books have episodes in which kids go back to the time of the dinosaurs, a guaranteed means for success in interesting reluctant readers. Don't forget the appeal of Michael Crichton's *Jurassic Park*. Other appealing dino titles include the following:

Arnold, Caroline. *Dinosaurs All Around: An Artist's View of the Prehistoric World*. How do artists create the models we see in museums?

Cole, Joanna. *The Magic School Bus in the Time of the Dinosaurs*. Lots of action and discovery as a class field trip into the time of dinosaurs turns into high adventure.

Davis, Lee. *Dinosaur Dinners* (Eyewitness Readers, Level 2). Primary-reading-level account of what dinos eat. Great glossary with pronunciation guide for adults too!

Dixon, Dougal. *Dougal Dixon's Dinosaurs*. 2nd Ed. All you wanted to know about dinosaurs and a bit more. Detailed illustrations and factual inserts.

Lindsay, William. *Tyrannosaurus*. Describes where these beasts lived, how we find remains of them and what their strengths as ferocious fighters were. Another book is about the greedy giant, the Barosaurus.

MacLeod, Elizabeth. *Dinosaurs: The Fastest, The Fiercest, The Most Amazing*. Which dino was the smartest, dumbest, laid the biggest egg, had the strangest tail, the thickest head or the longest horn? Large illustrations and simple text about each dino.

Taylor, Barbara. *The Really Deadly and Dangerous Dinosaur: And Other Monsters of the Prehistoric World*. Vibrant photos of models featuring terrible teeth, suits of armor, tearing talons, tail ends and other weaponry of these beasts.

---

*Reflection:*

This chapter is really about the right of reluctant readers to read what they want to—no matter what the subject. Just by being able to read, competent readers already have that freedom. As teachers of reluctant readers, we need to find out what they care about and not censor their choice, just because it is not our kind of book. It is a challenge to find out what reluctant readers are truly interested in, but with patience, experience and awareness, we can come closer each time. It is our job to find those books that get them involved and engaged in reading.

# Conclusion * Secrets to Success with Reluctant Readers

In this book we have explored the challenge of getting reluctant readers from grades three to six turned on to reading. It is clear that to read, we all must be motivated and willing to make time to read.

There are many types of reluctant readers, but all avoid the work of learning to read; each just finds a different way to do it. Some say they can't, some say they don't know how, some say they'd rather do something else and some say they don't want to try—ever. They are afraid to take risks, they think the material is too hard, they have other interests than reading or they perceive reading as being no use in the "real world." All reluctant readers are trying to avoid their fear of being wrong and fear of failure by denying the need to read.

We have found that certain reading materials and instruction methods work better with reluctant readers than others, for example: books and strategies that require them to become physically involved through manipulation; problem-solving, puzzle and game books that tease their minds into becoming involved; books that drag them into reading through personal interest; and, materials that are based in "real life" and help them deal with their image of the future. In general, successful strategies, activities and techniques should engage them through their bodies, their minds and their feelings. When these kids become engrossed, they will focus and be able to learn to read what they want.

We have also found that we can change reluctant readers' beliefs about themselves, and in so doing, change their reading ability. This can be done by:

- stopping doing the physical "work" of reading for them;
- putting choice into their hands and allowing them to feel power and control over reading;
- validating their emotional need to know through encouraging their interests no matter how different from our own;
- being conscious of the hidden curriculum and refocusing it to our reluctant readers' advantage;
- ruling "time" instead of letting time rule us and our reluctant readers;
- learning to approach reluctant readers with playful activities;
- being willing to engage them by reading aloud to them and by reading aloud together;
- sparking their imaginations through finding the best of whatever reluctant readers are willing to read, and then knowing other good books to take them to when they are ready;
- recognizing that media and computers are just other forms of reading;
- modeling through being readers ourselves.

As teachers of reluctant readers we must allow the richness, value and benefits of reading to shine through our modeling. What they see is what they will be.

Success with reluctant readers means we must focus on each reluctant reader as an individual who has different reading abilities and needs. We must be observant of physical behaviors, interpreting nuances in voice and manner and using this awareness to lead our instruction. We must let go of prescriptive curriculum and rigid instructional approaches; instead, we must lure our reluctant readers into finding the fun in reading and in sharing the jokes, puzzles and tricks inherent in our language. We must search for those perfect books, of whatever kind, that will engage our reluctant readers. Most of all, we must keep as our teaching motto:

*Go with the kids ... do whatever works!*

# Bibliography

## Print Titles

Ada, Alma Flor. *Yours Truly, Goldilocks.* Illustrated by Leslie Tryon. Atheneum, 1998.

Adler, David. *Cam Jansen and the Mystery of Flight 54* (A Cam Jansen Adventure). Illustrated by Susanna Natti. Viking, 1989.

Agee, Jon. *Go Hang a Salami. I'm A Lasagna Hog and Other Palindromes.* Farrar, Straus & Giroux, 1994.

Agee, Jon. *So Many Dynamos! And Other Palindromes.* Farrar, Straus & Giroux, 1994.

Ahlberg, Janet and Allan. *The Ha Ha Bonk Book.* Puffin, 1982.

Ahlberg, Janet and Allan. *It Was a Dark and Stormy Night.* Penguin, 1993.

Ainsworth, Ken. *Building a Solitaire Game and a Peg Board* (Building Together Series). Illustrated by Tina Holdcroft. Photography by Rodrigo Moreno. Annick, 1998.

Allen, Bob. *All Action Mountain Biking.* Lerner, 1991.

Allen, Eleanor. *Ghost Dog.* Scholastic, 1996.

Allen, Jonathan. *Wake Up, Sleeping Beauty! An Interactive Book with Sounds.* Dial, 1997.

Alles, Hemesh, illus. *Errata: A Book of Historical Errors.* Written by S.A.J. Wood. Green Tiger/Simon & Schuster, 1992.

Amato, Carol. *Captain Jim and the Killer Whales* (Young Readers' Series). Illustrated by Patrick O'Brien. Barron's, 1995.

Anderson, Kevin J. and Rebecca Moesta. *Star Wars Young Jedi Knights: Diversity Alliance.* Boulevard Books, 1997.

Anderson, Scoular. *A Puzzling Day in the Land of the Pharoahs: A Search-and-Solve Gamebook.* Candlewick, 1996.

Anno, Mitsumasa. *Anno's Alphabet: An Adventure in Imagination.* Crowell, 1975.

Anno, Mitsumasa. *Anno's Counting Book.* Crowell, 1977.

Anno, Mitsumasa. *Anno's Journey.* Philomel, 1981.

Appelt, Kathi. *Bat Jamboree.* Illustrated by Melissa Sweet. Morrow, 1998.

Arnold, Caroline. *Bat.* Photography by Richard Hewett. Morrow, 1996.
Arnold, Caroline. *Cats in from the Wild.* Photography by Richard R. Hewett. Carolrhoda, 1993.
Arnold, Caroline. *Dinosaurs All Around: An Artist's View of the Prehistoric World.* Photography by Richard Hewett. Clarion, 1993.
Arnold, Caroline. *Monkey.* Photography by Richard Hewett. Morrow, 1993.
Arthur, Robert. *The Mystery of the Green Ghost* (The Three Investigators). Random House, 1998.
Ash, Russell. *Incredible Comparison.* Dorling Kindersley, 1996.
Ash, Russell. *The Top Ten of Everything.* Reader's Digest, 1997.
Auch, Mary Jane. *Peeping Beauty.* Holiday House, 1993.
Avi. *City of Light, City of Dark: A Comic-Book Novel.* Illustrated by Brian Floca. Orchard, 1995.
Awan, Shaila, ed. *Monster Machines.* Scholastic, 1998.

Babbitt, Natalie. *Tuck Everlasting.* Farrar, Straus & Giroux, 1975.
Bailey, Linda. *How Come the Best Clues Are Always in the Garbage?* (A Stevie Diamond Mystery). Kids Can Press/Puffin, 1992.
Baker, Jeannie. *The Story of Rosy Dock.* Greenwillow, 1995.
Baker, Jeannie. *Where the Forest Meets the Sea.* Greenwillow, 1987.
Baker, Jeannie. *Window.* Greenwillow, 1991.
Baker, Lucy. *Life in the Deserts: Animals, People, Plants.* Scholastic, 1990.
Ballie, Allan. *Dragon Quest.* Illustrated by Wayne Harris. Scholastic, 1996.
Banks, Lynne Reid. *Harry the Poisonous Centipede: A Story to Make You Squirm.* Illustrated by Tony Ross. Morrow, 1997.
Banyai, Istvan. *Zoom.* Penguin, 1995.
Base, Grahame. *Animalia.* Abrams, 1987.
Bauer, Marion. *Alison's Wings* (Hyperion Chapters). Illustrated by Roger Roth. Hyperion, 1996.
Bayer, June. *A, My Name is ALICE.* Illustrated by Steven Kellogg. Dial, 1984.
Bayley, Nicola. *The Necessary Cat.* Candlewick, 1998.
Bell, William. *Crabbe.* Little Brown, 1987.
Bell, William. *Forbidden City.* Doubleday Canada, 1990.
Berger, Melvin. *One Hundred and One Spooky Halloween Jokes.* Scholastic, 1993.
Betancourt, Jeanne. *The Missing Pony Pal* (Pony Pals). Scholastic, 1997.
Betz, Adrienne. *Treasury of Quotations for Children.* Scholastic, 1998.
Biesty, Stephen. *Castle* (Stephen Biesty's Cross-Sections). Dorling Kindersley, 1994.
Bingham, Caroline. *Big Rig* (Mighty Machines). Dorling Kindersley, 1996.
Bingham, Caroline. *Race Car* (Mighty Machines). Dorling Kindersley, 1996.
Birmingham, Duncan. *"M" is for Mirror.* Tarquin, 1988.
Blake, Quentin, ed. *Quentin Blake's Book of Nonsense Stories.* Viking, 1996.
Blyton, Enid. *Castle of Adventure* (Adventure Series). Macmillan 1947/1988.
Bodkin, Odds. *The Crane Wife.* Illustrated by Gennady Spirin. Gulliver/Harcourt Brace, 1998.
*The Bones and Skeleton Book: Get to Know Your Body from the Inside Out.* Workman.
Boniface, William. *Mystery in Bugtown.* Illustrated by Jim Harris. Accord, 1977.
Bonson, Richard and Richard Platt. *Disaster! Catastrophes That Shook the World.* Viking, 1997.
Branford, Henrietta. *Dimanche Diller.* Illustrated by Lesley Harker. Galaxy, 1995.

Branzei, Sylvia. *Planet Dexter's Grossology: Gross Science That Kids Want to Learn.* Addison Wesley, 1995.

Brenner, Barbara. *Thinking About Ants.* Illustrated by Carol Schwartz. Mondo, 1997.

Brett, Jan. *The First Dog.* Harcourt Brace, 1988.

Brewster, Hugh. *Anastasia's Album: The Last Tsar's Youngest Daughter Tells Her Own Story.* Penguin/Madison, 1996.

Briggs, Raymond. *The Man.* Random House, 1992.

Briggs, Raymond. *The Snowman.* Random House, 1978.

Brooks, Alan. *Frogs Jump: A Counting Book.* Illustrated by Steven Kellogg. Scholastic, 1996.

Brooks, Bruce. *Billy* (The Wolfbay Wings, #7). HarperCollins, 1998.

Brooks, Bruce. *Cody* (The Wolfbay Wings, #3). HarperCollins, 1997.

Brooks, Bruce. *Zip* (The Wolfbay Wings, #2). HarperCollins, 1997.

Brown, Marc. *Arthur Makes the Team* (Arthur Chapter Books, #3). Little Brown, 1998.

Brown, Marc. *Scared Silly! A Book for the Brave: Poems, Riddles, Jokes, Stories and More.* Little Brown, 1994.

Brown, Ruth. *If at First You Do Not See.* Holt, 1982.

Brown, Ruth. *The World That Jack Built.* Anderson, 1990.

Browne, Anthony. *Willy the Wimp.* Julia MacRae, 1984/ Knopf, 1989.

Bryan, Ashley. *The Cat's Purr.* Atheneum, 1985.

Bryant, Bonnie. *English Horse* (The Saddle Club, #79). Bantam, 1998.

Buck, Nola. *Creepy Crawly Critters: And Other Halloween Tongue Twisters.* HarperCollins, 1995.

Budd, Jackie. *Horses.* Kingfisher, 1995.

Bunting, Eve. *A Day's Work.* Illustrated by Ronald Himler. Clarion, 1994.

Bunting, Eve. *Fly Away Home.* Illustrated by Ronald Himler. Clarion, 1991.

Bunting, Eve. *How Many Days to America: A Thanksgiving Story.* Illustrated by Beth Peck. Clarion, 1990.

Bunting, Eve. *Nasty, Stinky Sneakers.* HarperCollins, 1995.

Bunting, Eve. *Smoky Night.* Illustrated by David Diaz. Harcourt Brace, 1994.

Bunting. Eve. *Train to Somewhere.* Illustrated by Ronald Himler. Clarion, 1996.

Bunting, Eve. *The Wall.* Illustrated by Ronald Himler. Clarion, 1988.

Bunting, Eve. *Your Move.* Illustrated by James Ransome. Harcourt Brace, 1998.

Burston, Patrick. *The Planet of Terror* (A Choose Your Challenge Gamebook). Illustrated by Allastair Graham. Candlewick, 1985/1996.

Butterfield, Moira. *Record Breakers* (Look Inside Cross-Sections). Illustrated by Chris Grigg and Keith Harmer. Scholastic Canada/Dorling Kindersley, 1995.

Byars, Betsy. *Pinballs.* HarperCollins, 1977.

Byars, Betsy. *Tornado* (A Trophy Chapter Book). Illustrated by Doron Ben-Ami. HarperCollins, 1996.

Calhoun, Mary. *Cross-Country Cat.* Illustrated by Erick Ingraham. Morrow, 1986.

Calmenson, Stephanie and Joanna Cole. *The Gator Girls: Rockin' Reptiles* (Beech Tree Chapter Books). Illustrated by Lynn Munsinger. Beech Tree, 1997.

Campbell, Joanna. *Stirlings' Second Chance* (Thoroughbred Series #26). HarperCollins, 1998.

Cannon, Janell. *Stellaluna.* Harcourt Brace, 1993.

Cannon, Janell. *Verdi.* Harcourt Brace, 1997.

Carle, Eric. *Hello, Red Fox.* Simon & Schuster, 1998.

Cassidy, John. *Earthsearch: A Kid's Geography Museum in a Book.* Klutz, 1994.

Cassidy, John. *Explorabook: A Kid's Science Museum in a Book.* Klutz, 1991.

Cassidy, John. *The Klutz Book of Knots.* Klutz, 1985.

Cassidy, John and Michael Stroud. *The Klutz Book of Magic.* Illustrated by H.B. Lewis and Sara Boore. Klutz, 1990.

Christensen, Bonnie. *Rebus Riot.* Dial, 1997.

Christopher, Matt. *Baseball Jokes and Riddles.* Illustrated by Dan Vasconsellos. Little Brown, 1996.

Christopher, Matt. *Dirt Bike Racer.* Little Brown, 1979.

Christopher, Matt. *Dirt Bike Runaway.* Little Brown, 1983.

Christopher, Matt. *Ice Magic.* Little Brown, 1973.

Christopher, Matt. *The Lucky Baseball Bat.* Illustrated by Dee deRosa. Little Brown, 1991.

Christopher, Matt. *Shoot for the Hoop.* Little Brown, 1963/1995.

Christopher, Matt. *Skateboard Tough.* Little Brown, 1991.

Christopher, Matt. *Snowboard Maverick.* Little Brown, 1997.

Civardi, Anne et al. *The Usborne Detective's Handbook.* Illustrated by Colin King. Usborne, 1979.

Clark, Margaret and Phil Hayes. *Meatball's Good Dog Day.* Mark MacLeod/Random House, 1998.

Cleary, Beverly. *Dear Mr. Henshaw.* Illustrated by Paul Zelinski. Morrow, 1983.

Cleary, Beverly. *Lucky Chuck.* Illustrated by J. Winslow Higginbottom. Morrow, 1984.

Cleary, Beverly. *The Mouse and the Motorcycle.* Illustrated by Louis Darling. Morrow, 1965.

Cleary, Beverly. *Muggie Maggie.* Morrow, 1993.

Cleary, Beverly. *Ramona and Her Father.* Illustrated by Alan Tiegreen. Morrow, 1977.

Cleary, Beverly. *Ramona the Pest.* Illustrated by Louis Darling. Morrow, 1968.

Cleary, Beverly. *Runaway Ralph.* Illustrated by Louis Darling. Morrow, 1970.

Cleary, Beverly. *Socks.* Illustrated by Beatrice Darwin. Morrow, 1973.

Clutton-Brock, Juliet. *Cat.* Stoddart/Dorling Kindersley, 1991.

Coerr, Eleanor. *Sadako.* Illustrated by Ed Young. Putnam, 1993.

Coerr, Eleanor. *Sadako and the Thousand Paper Cranes.* Illustrated by Ron Himler. Putnam, 1977.

Cole, Joanna and Stephanie Calmenson. *Crazy Eights and Other Card Games.* Illustrated by Alan Tiegren. Beech Tree, 1994.

Cole, Joanna and Stephanie Calmenson. *Marbles: 101 Ways to Play.* Illustrated by Alan Tiegreen. Morrow, 1998.

Cole, Joanna. *In the Time of the Dinosaurs* (The Magic School Bus). Illustrated by Bruce Degen. Scholastic, 1994.

Cole, Joanna. *Inside a Beehive* (The Magic School Bus). Illustrated by Bruce Degen. Scholastic, 1996.

Cole, Joanna. *Inside a Hurricane* (The Magic School Bus). Illustrated by Bruce Degen. Scholastic, 1996.

Cole, Joanna. *Inside the Earth* (The Magic School Bus). Illustrated by Bruce Degen. Scholastic, 1989.

Cole, Joanna. *Inside the Human Body* (The Magic School Bus). Illustrated by Bruce Degen. Scholastic, 1990.

Cole, Joanne. *Monster Manners* (Hellow Readers!). Illustrated by Jared Lee. Scholastic, 1985.

Coleman, Michael. *Internet Detectives: Speed Surf*. Bantam, 1997.

Collington, Peter. *A Small Miracle*. Knopf, 1997.

Conford, Ellen. *A Case for Jenny Archer*. Illustrated by Diane Palmisciano. Little Brown, 1988.

Conrad, Pam. *Staying Nine* (A Trophy Chapter Book). Illustrated by Mike Wimmer. HarperCollins, 1988.

Cooney, Caroline. *Face on the Milk Carton*. Dell, 1991.

Cooney, Caroline. *Whatever Happened to Janie?* Delacorte, 1993.

Cooper, Floyd. *Cumbayah*. Morrow, 1998.

Cooper, Susan. *The Boggart*. McElderry/Atheneum, 1993.

*The Cootie Catcher Book*. Klutz, 1997.

Cosby, Bill. *The Meanest Thing to Say* (Little Bill Books for Beginning Readers). Illustrated by Varnette P. Honeywood. Scholastic, 1997.

Coville, Bruce and Katherine. *Sarah's Unicorn*. HarperCollins, 1979.

Coville, Bruce. *Aliens Ate My Homework*. Illustrated by Katherine Coville. Pocket, 1993.

Creech, Sharon. *Walk Two Moons*. HarperCollins, 1994.

Crew, Gary. *The Watertower*. Illustrated by Steven Woolman. Era, 1994/Interlink, 1997.

Croll, Carolyn. *Too Many Babas* (An I Can Read Book). HarperCollins, 1979/1994.

Cushman, Doug. *The Mystery of King Karfu*. HarperCollins, 1996.

Cushman, Karen. *Catherine, Called Birdy*. Clarion, 1994.

Cushman, Karen. *The Midwife's Apprentice*. Clarion, 1995.

Cyrus, Kurt. *Tangle Town*. Farrar, Straus & Giroux, 1998.


Dadey, Debbie and Marcia Jones. *Hercules Doesn't Pull Teeth* (The Adventures of the Bailey School Kids, #30). Scholastic, 1998.

Dahl, Roald. *The BFG*. Illustrated by Quentin Blake. Farrar, Straus & Giroux, 1982.

Dahl, Roald. *Charlie and the Chocolate Factory*. Illustrated by Joseph Schindelman. Knopf, 1964.

Dahl, Roald. *James and the Giant Peach*. Illustrated by Lane Smith. Knopf, 1996.

Dahl, Roald. *Matilda*. Illustrated by Quentin Blake. Viking, 1988.

Dahl, Roald. *The Witches*. Illustrated by Quentin Blake. Farrar, Straus & Giroux, 1983.

Danziger, Paula. *Amber Brown is Not a Crayon*. Illustrated by Tony Ross. Putnam, 1994.

Danziger, Paula. *There's a Bat in Bunk Five*. Dell, 1988.

Davis, Lee. *Dinosaur Dinners* (Eyewitness Readers). Dorling Kindersley, 1998.

Day, Alexandra. *Good Dog, Carl*. Green Tiger/Simon & Schuster, 1985.

De Paola, Tomie. *Pancakes for Breakfast*. Harcourt Brace, 1978.

De Paola, Tomie. *Tomie de Paola's Book of Poems*. Putnam, 1988.

De Regniers, Beatrice Schenk, ed. *Sing a Song of Popcorn*. Scholastic, 1988.

Delafosse, Claude. *Animals* (A First Discovery Art Book). Illustrated by Tony Ross. Cartwheel Books/ Scholastic, 1995.

Delton, Judy. *Pee Wee Scouts: Pedal Power*. Illustrated by Alan Tiegren. BDD Yearling, 1998.

Dewin, Ted, illus. *Inside the Whale and Other Animals*. Dorling Kindersley/Scholastic Canada, 1992.

Dicks, Ian and David Hawcock. *Unwrap the Mummy! A Four-foot-long, Fact-filled, Pop-up Mummy to Explore!* Random House, 1995.

*Dinosaur Hunt: A Pull-out, Pop-up Discovery*. Illustrated by Philip Hood. Putnam & Grosset, 1995.

Dixon, Andy. *Sword Quest* (A Fantasy Adventure Games Series). Illustrated by Simone Boni. Usborne, 1997/ EDC, 1997.

Dixon, Dougal. *Dougal Dixon's Dinosaurs. 2nd Ed.* Boyds Mills, 1993.

Donnelly, Judy. *The Titanic Lost ... and Found* (STEP into Reading). Illustrated by Keith Kohler. Random House, 1987.

Donnelly, Judy. *True-Life Treasure Hunts* (STEP into Reading). Illustrated by Thomas La Padula. Random House, 1983/1994.

Dougall, Alastair, ed. *Essential Facts*. Firefly, 1996.

Drake, Jane and Ann Love. *The Kids Cottage Games Book*. Illustrated by Heather Collins. Kids Can, 1998.

Ducy, K. and K.A. Bale. *Survival, The Titanic, April 14, 1912* (Survival! Series). Aladdin/Simon & Schuster, 1998.

Dunphy, Madeleine. *Here is the Wetland*. Illustrated by Wayne McLoughlin. Hyperion, 1996.

Duplacey, James. *Great Goalies* (NHL Hockey Superstars). Kids Can/Morrow, 1996.

Duplacey, James. *Top Rookies* (NHL Hockey Superstars). Kids Can/Morrow, 1996.

Eckstein, Joan and Joyce Gleit. *The Best Joke Book for Kids*. Illustrated by J. Behr. Avon, 1977.

Edwards, Elwyn Hartley. *Horse: A Visual Guide to over 100 Horse Breeds from around the World* (Eyewitness Handbook). Stoddart/Dorling Kindersley, 1993.

Edwards, Pamela Duncan. *Four Famished Foxes and Fosdyke*. Illustrated by Henry Cole. HarperCollins, 1995.

Ehrlich, Fred. *Lunch Boxes* (Puffin Easy-to-Read). Illustrated by Martha Gradisher. Penguin, 1993.

Else, George. *Insects and Spiders* (The Nature Company Discovery Library). Time Life Books, 1997.

Emberley, Barbara. *Drummer Hoff*. Illustrated by Ed Emberley. Aladdin, 1972.

Enderle, Judith and Stephanie Tessler. *What's the Matter, Kelly Beans?* Illustrated by Blanche Sims. Candlewick, 1996.

Evans, Mark. *Kitten: A Practical Guide to Caring for Your Kitten* (ASPCA Pet Care Guides For Kids Series). Dorling Kindersley, 1993.

Evans, Mark. *Puppy: A Practical Guide to Caring for Your Puppy* (ASPCA Pet Care Guides For Kids Series). Dorling Kindersley, 1993.

Everts, Tammy and Bobbie Kalman. *Horses*. Crabtree, 1995.

Falwell, Cathryn. *Word Wizard*. Clarion, 1998.

Farmer, Nancy. *The Ear, the Eye and the Arm*. Orchard, 1995.

Feiffer, Jules. *A Barrel of Laughs, a Vale of Tears*. Michael diCapua/HarperCollins, 1995.

Feiffer, Jules. *Meanwhile....* Michael diCapua/HarperCollins, 1997.

Fine, Anne. *The Diary of a Killer Cat*. Illustrated by Steve Cox. Hamish Hamilton, 1994/Puffin, 1996.

Fison, Josie and Felicity Dahl. *Roald Dahl's Revolting Recipes*. Illustrated by Quentin Blake. Jonathan Cape, 1994.

Fitch, Sheree. *There's A Mouse in My House!* Illustrated by Leslie E. Watts. Doubleday Canada, 1997.

Fitzhugh, Louise. *Harriet, the Spy.* HarperCollins, 1964.

Fleischman, Paul. *Joyful Noise: Poems for Two Voices.* Illustrated by Eric Beddows. HarperCollins, 1992.

Fleischman, Sid. *McBroom's Wonderful One-Acre Farm* (Beech Tree Chapter Books). Pictures by Quentin Blake. Beech Tree, 1992.

Fleming, Denise. *In the Tall, Tall Grass.* Holt, 1991.

Folsom, Marcia and Michael. *Easy as Pie: A Guessing Game of Sayings.* Pictures by Jack Kent. Clarion, 1985.

Fornari, Giuliano. *Inside the Body* (A Lift-the-Flap Book). Fenn, 1996.

Fox, Paula. *The Eagle Kite.* Orchard, 1995.

Fox, Paula. *Monkey Island.* Orchard, 1991.

French, Fiona. *Snow White in New York.* Oxford, 1992.

*Fun With Your Cat: A Science Kit.* Scientific Explorer, 1997.

Geisert, Arthur. *Pigs from A to Z.* Houghton Mifflin, 1986.

George, Jean Craighead. *The Cry of the Crow.* HarperCollins, 1980.

George, Jean Craighead. *Julie of the Wolves.* Illustrated by John Schoenherr. HarperCollins, 1972.

George, Jean Craighead. *My Side of the Mountain.* Dutton, 1959.

George, Jean Craighead. *The Tarantula in My Purse and 172 Other Wild Pets.* HarperCollins, 1997.

George, Twig. C. *A Dolphin Named Bob* (A Trophy Chapter Book). Illustrated by Christine Herman Merrill. HarperCollins, 1996.

Gerstein, Mordicai. *The New Creatures.* HarperCollins, 1991.

Gilson, Jamie. *It Goes Eeeeeeeeeeee!* Illustrated by Diane Groat. Clarion, 1994.

Gleitzman, Morris. *Blabber Mouth.* Harcourt Brace, 1995.

Godfrey, Martin. *Here She Is—Ms. Teeny Wonderful.* Scholastic Canada, 1985.

Golden, Christopher. *The Empire Strikes Back* (Choose Your Own Star Wars Adventure). Illustrated by Phil Franké. Bantam, 1998.

Golden, Christopher. *Return of the Jedi* (Choose Your Own Star Wars Adventure). Illustrated by Phil Franké. Bantam, 1998.

Golden, Christopher. *The 10-Minute Detective: 25 Scene-of-the-Crime Mystery Puzzles You Can Solve Yourself.* Prima, 1997.

Goodall, Jane. *The Chimpanzee Family Book.* North South, 1989.

Goodall, John. *The Story of an English Village.* Macmillan, 1978.

Graham, Ian. *Racing Cars* (How It Goes). Barron's, 1994.

Gralla, Preston. *Online Kids: A Young Surfer's Guide to Cyberspace.* Wiley, 1996.

Granfield, Linda. *In Flanders Fields: The Story of the Poem by John McCrae.* Bantam Dell Doubleday, 1996.

Gray, Libba Moore. *Small Green Snake.* Illustrated by Holly Meade. Orchard, 1994.

Greenaway, Theresa. *The Really Hairy Scary Spider and Other Creatures With Lots of Legs.* Photography by Frank Greenaway and Kim Taylor. Dorling Kindersley, 1996.

Greenburg, Dan. *Never Trust a Cat Who Wears Earrings* (The Zack Files). Illustrated by Jack E. Davis. Grosset & Dunlap, 1997.

Griffith, Helen. *Foxy.* Greenwillow, 1984.

Grislis, Peter. *The Calligraphy Book.* Scholastic, 1988.

Gryski, Camilla. *Camilla Gryski's Favourite String Games.* Kids Can, 1995.

Gryski, Camilla. *Cat's Cradle, Owl's Eyes: A Book of String Games*. Illustrated by Tom Sankey. Morrow, 1984.

Gryski, Camilla. *Hands On, Thumbs Up*. Illustrated by Pat Cupples. Kids Can, 1990/Addison-Wesley, 1991.

Gryski, Camilla. *Many Stars and More String Games*. Illustrated by Tom Sankey. Morrow, 1985.

Gryski, Camilla. *Super String Games*. Illustrated by Tom Sankey. Kids Can Press, 1987/Morrow, 1988.

*The Guinness Book of Records*. Guinness, 1998.

Gwynne, Fred. *Chocolate Moose for Dinner*. Simon & Schuster, 1988.

Hall, Katy and Lisa Eisenberg. *Fishy Riddles*. Illustrated by Simms Taback. Dial, 1983/ Puffin, 1993.

Hall, Katy and Lisa Eisenberg. *Mummy Riddles*. Dial, 1997.

Hall, Katy and Lisa Eisenberg. *One Hundred One Cat and Dog Jokes*. Scholastic, 1990.

Hall, Katy and Lisa Eisenberg. *Sheepish Riddles*. Illustrated by R.W. Alley. Dial, 1997.

Hall, Lynn. *Barry: The Bravest Saint Bernard* (STEP into Reading). Illustrated by Antonio Castro. Random House, 1973/1992.

Handford, Martin. *Where's Waldo? 2nd Ed.* Candlewick, 1997.

Handford, Martin. *Where's Waldo? In Hollywood*. Candlewick, 1994.

Handford, Martin. *Where's Waldo? The Fantastic Journey*. Candlewick, 1997.

Handford, Martin. *Where's Waldo Now? 2nd Ed.* Candlewick, 1997.

Hanrahan, Brendan. *Meet the Chicago Bulls*. Scholastic, 1996.

Harper, Piers. *Snakes and Ladders and Hundreds of Mice!* Candlewick, 1997.

Harris, Nicholas. *Into the Rain Forest* (The Nature Company EcoXplorer Series). Illustrated by Eric Robson. Orpheus/Time Life, 1996.

Harris, Peter. *Have You Seen Max!* Illustrated by Korky Paul. Aladdin, 1994.

Harris, Peter. *Mouse Creeps*. Illustrated by Reg Cartwright. WH Books, 1997.

Harvey, Ian. *Tanks* (Look Inside Cross-Sections). Illustrated by Richard Chasemore. Scholastic Canada/Dorling Kindersley, 1996.

Haskins, Lori. *Breakout! Escape from Alcatraz* (STEP into Reading). Illustrated by Janet Hamlin. Random House, 1996.

Hathorn, Libby. *Way Home*. Illustrated by Gregory Rogers. Mark MacLeod/ Random House, 1994.

Hawcock, David. *The Amazing Pop-up, Pull-out Space Shuttle*. Press élan, 1998.

Heidbreder, Robert. *Eenie Meenie Manitoba*. Illustrated by Scot Ritchie. Kids Can Press, 1996.

Heller, Ruth. *A Cache of Jewels and Other Collective Nouns*. Grossett & Dunlap, 1987.

Heller, Ruth. *Many Luscious Lollipops: A Book About Adjectives*. Grosset & Dunlap, 1989.

Heneghan, Jim. *The Trail of the Chocolate Thief*. Scholastic Canada, 1993.

Henkes, Kevin. *Lily's Purple Plastic Purse*. Greenwillow, 1996.

Hepworth, Cathi. *Bug Off!* Putnam, 1998.

Heywood, Rosie. *The Great City Search*. Illustrated by David Hancock. Usborne, 1997.

Himmelman, John. *The Animal Rescue Club* (An I Can Read Chapter Book). HarperCollins, 1998.

*The History of Making Books* (A Scholastic Voyages of Discovery Book). Scholastic, 1995.

Hoban, Tana. *Just Look*. Greenwillow, 1996.

Hobbs, Will. *Beardance*. Atheneum, 1993.

Hockman, Hilary, ed. *What's Inside? Everyday Things*. Grolier, 1992.

Hodge, Deborah. *Wild Cats: Cougars, Bobcats and Lynx*. Illustrated by Nancy Gray Ogle. Kids Can, 1997.

Holman, Felice. *Slake's Limbo*. Scribner's, 1994.

Holzwarth, Werner. *The Story of the Little Mole Who Knew It Was None of His Business*. Illustrated by Wolf Erlbruch. Raincoast, 1994.

Hooks, William. *Lo-Jack and the Pirates* (Bank Street Ready-to-Read). Illustrated by Tricia Tusa. Bantam, 1991.

Houston, James. *Frozen Fire*. Atheneum, 1977.

Howe, James. *Bunnicula Escapes! A Pop-up Adventure*. Illustrated by Alan and Lea Daniel. Morrow, 1994.

Howe, James. *I Wish I Were a Butterfly*. Illustrated by Ed Young. Harcourt Brace, 1987.

Hughes, Monica. *The Golden Aquarians*. HarperCollins, 1994.

Hughes, Monica. *Hunter in the Dark*. Avon, 1984/ Stoddart Kids, 1993.

Hughes, Monica. *The Keeper of the Isis Light*. Nelson, 1980.

Iguchi, Bryan. *The Young Snowboarder*. Stoddart/Dorling Kindersley, 1997.

Imes, Rick. *Incredible Bugs: An Eye-Opening Guide to the Amazing World of Insects*. Macmillan Canada, 1997.

Innocenti, Roberto. *Rose Blanche*. Harcourt Brace, 1996.

Jackson, Ellen. *Cinder Edna*. Illustrated by Kevin O'Malley. Lothrop Lee & Shepard, 1994.

Jackson, Ellen. *Turn of the Century*. Illustrated by Jan Davey. Ellis Charlesbridge, 1998.

Jacques, Brian. *Mossflower*. Illustrated by Gary Chalk. Putnam, 1988.

Jacques, Brian. *Outcast of Redwall: A Tale from Redwall*. Illustrated by Gary Chalk. Putnam, 1996.

Jacques, Brian. *Redwall*. Illustrated by Gary Chalk. Putnam, 1987.

Jennings, Paul, Ted Greenwood and Terry Denton. *Freeze A Crowd*. Viking, 1996.

Jennings, Paul. *Unreal!* Penguin, 1985.

Jewell, Nancy. *Silly Times with Two Silly Trolls* (An I Can Read Book). Illustrated by Lisa Thiesing. HarperCollins, 1996.

Johnson, Stephen T. *City by Numbers*. Viking, 1998.

Johnson, Stephen. T. *Alphabet City*. Viking, 1995.

Johnson, Sylvia A. *Bats*. Photography by Modoki Masuda. Lerner, 1985.

Johnston, Julie. *Adam and Eve and Pinch Me*. Little Brown, 1993.

Jonas, Ann. *The 13th Clue*. Dell, 1992.

Joyce, Susan. *Alphabet Riddles*. Illustrations by Doug DuBosque. Peel Productions, 1998.

Karr, Kathleen. *The Lighthouse Mermaid* (Hyperion Chapters). Illustrated by Karen Lee Schmidt. Hyperion, 1998.

Kawakami, Kenji. *99 More Unuseless Japanese Inventions: The Art of Chindogu*. Translated from the Japanese by Dan Paia. HarperCollins, 1997.

Keens-Douglas, Richardo. *Freedom Child of the Sea*. Illustrated by Julia Gukova. Annick, 1995.

Kellogg, Stephen. *The Day Jimmy's Boa Ate the Wash*. Dial, 1980.

Kellogg, Stephen. *The Island Of Skogg*. Dial, 1973.

Kellogg, Stephen. *Mysterious Tadpole*. Dial, 1979.

Kellogg, Stephen. *Paul Bunyan*. Morrow, 1984.

Kellogg, Stephen. *Pecos Bill*. Morrow, 1986.

Kellogg, Stephen. *A Rose for Pinkerton*. Dial, 1981.

Kennedy, X.J. *Brats*. Illustrated by James Watts. McElderry/Simon & Schuster, 1986.

Kent, Peter. *Hidden Under the Ground: The World Beneath Your Feet*. Scholastic, 1998.

Ketteman, Helen. *Buba the Cowboy Prince: A Fractured Texas Tale*. Illustrated by James Warhola. Scholastic, 1997.

Khanduri, Kamini. *The Great World Tour*. Illustrated by David Hancock. Usborne, 1997.

Kidd, Diana. *Onion Tears*. Illustrated by Lucy Montgomery. Orchard, 1991.

*The Kids' Question and Answer Book*. From the Editors of Owl Magazine. Grosset & Dunlap, 1988.

*KidsCooking: A Very Slightly Messy Manual*. Illustrated by Jim M'Guinness. Klutz, 1987.

Kindersley, Barnabas and Anabel. *Celebrations!* (Children Just Like Me). Dorling Kindersley, 1997.

King-Smith, Dick. *Babe: The Gallant Pig*. Illustrated by Mary Rayner. Harcourt Brace, 1994.

Knowles, Sheena. *Edward the Emu*. Illustrated by Rod Clement. HarperCollins, 1988.

Korman, Gordon and Bernice. *The Last-Place Sports Poems of Jeremy Bloom*. Scholastic, 1996.

Korman, Gordon. *The Chicken Doesn't Skate*. Scholastic, 1996.

Korman, Gordon. *The Zucchini Warriors*. Scholastic, 1991.

Kranz, Linda. *All About ME: A Keepsake Journal for Kids*. Whitecap Books, 1996.

Kroeger, Mary Kay and Louise Borden. *Paperboy*. Illustrated by Ted Lewin. Clarion, 1996.

Kruger, Anna, ed. *The Dorling Kindersley Visual Encyclopedia*. Dorling Kindersley, 1995.


L'Engle, Madeleine. *A Wrinkle in Time*. Farrar, Straus & Giroux, 1962.

Laden, Nina. *Private I. Iguana: The Case of the Missing Chameleon*. Chronicle, 1995.

Laden, Nina. *The Night I Followed the Dog*. Chronicle, 1994.

Laden, Nina. *When Pigasso Met Mootisse*. Chronicle, 1998.

Lambert, David. *Dinosaur! Build Your Own Model Triceratops from the Inside Out and Discover a Lost World!* (Science Action Book). Running Press, 1998.

Langley, Andrew and Philip de Souza. *The Roman News*. Candlewick, 1996.

Larrick, Nancy, ed. *Cats Are Cats: Poems*. Drawings by Ed Young. Philomel, 1988.

Larson, Kirby. *Sitting in a Tree* (Cody and Quinn). Drawings by Nancy Poydar. Bantam Doubleday Dell, 1996.

Lasky, Kathryn. *Grace the Pirate* (Hyperion Chapters). Illustrated by Karen Lee Schmidt. Hyperion, 1997.

Lattimore, Deborah Nourse. *I Wonder What's Under There? A Brief History of*

*Underwear.* (A Lift-the-Flap Book). Paper Engineering by David A. Carter. Browndeer/Harcourt Brace, 1998.

Lauber, Patricia. *The True-or-False Book of Cats.* Illustrated by Rosslyn Schanzer. National Geographic Society, 1998.

Layden, Joe. *Meet the Los Angeles Lakers.* Scholastic, 1997.

Leach, Maria. *Whistle in the Graveyard: Folktales to Chill Your Bones.* Viking, 1974.

Lesynski, Loris. *Catmagic.* Annick, 1998.

Leverich, Kathleen. *Best Enemies Forever.* Illustrated by Walter Lorraine. Beech Tree, 1995.

Levine, Arthur A. *Pearl Moscowitz's Last Stand.* Pictures by Robert Roth. Tambourine, 1993.

Levinson, Nancy Smiler. *Snowshoe Thompson* (An I Can Read Book). Pictures by Joan Sandin. HarperCollins, 1992.

Levithan, David. *In the Eye of the Tornado* (Disaster Zone Books). Scholastic, 1998.

Levithan, David. *In the Heart of the Quake* (Disaster Zone Books). Scholastic, 1998.

Levy, Elizabeth. *Dracula Is a Pain in the Neck* (A Trophy Chapter Book). Illustrated by Mordicai Gerstein. HarperCollins, 1983.

Levy, Elizabeth. *Frankenstein Moves in on the Fourth Floor* (A Trophy Chapter Book). HarperCollins, 1979.

Lewis, C.S. *The Lion, the Witch and the Wardrobe.* Illustrated by Pauline Baynes. HarperCollins, 1994/1950.

Lewis, J. Patrick. *Doodle Dandies: Poems That Take Shape.* Images by Lisa Desimini. Atheneum, 1998.

Lewis, J. Patrick. *The House of Boo.* Illustrated by Katya Krénina. Atheneum, 1998.

Lindsay, William. *The Natural History Museum: Tyrannosaurus.* Stoddart, 1992/ Dorling Kindersley, 1992.

Ling, M. *Amazing Wolves, Dogs and Foxes* (Amazing Worlds Series). Stoddart, 1991.

Ling, Mary and Mary Atkinson. *The Snake Book.* Photography by Rank Greenaway and Dave King. Dorling Kindersley, 1997.

Ling, Mary. *Wild Animal Go-Round: Turn the Wheel and See the Animals Grow.* Dorling Kindersley, 1995.

Linton, Marilyn. *Just Desserts and Other Treats for Kids to Make.* Illustrated by Barbara Reid. Kids Can, 1998.

Little, Emily. *The Trojan Horse: How the Greeks Won the War* (STEP into Reading). Illustrated by Michael Eagle. Random House, 1988.

Little, Jean and Maggie de Vries. *Once Upon a Golden Apple.* Illustrated by Phoebe Gilman. Viking, 1991.

Little, Jean. *Different Dragons.* Illustrated by Laura Fernandez. Viking, 1989.

Little, Jean. *From Anna.* Illustrated by Joan Sandin. HarperCollins, 1972.

Little, Jean. *Mine for Keeps.* Little Brown, 1962/Viking, 1994.

Llewellyn, Claire. *The Best Book of Bugs.* Kingfisher, 1998.

Llewellyn, Claire. *Tractor* (Mighty Machines). Dorling Kindersley, 1995.

Llewellyn, Claire. *Truck* (Mighty Machines). Dorling Kindersley, 1995.

Lobel, Arnold. *Fables.* HarperCollins, 1980.

Louie, Ai-Ling. *Yeh Shen: A Cinderella Story from China.* Illustrated by Ed Young. Philomel, 1982.

Lovka, Bob. *The Splendid Little Book of All Things Cat*. Illustrated by Setsu Broderick. Bowtie Press, 1998.

Lowell, Melissa. *Silver Blades on the Edge* (Gold Medal Dreams, #1). Skylark/Bantam Doubleday Dell, 1997.

Lowry, Lois. *Anastasia Absolutely*. Houghton Mifflin, 1995.

Lowry, Lois. *Anastasia, Ask Your Analyst*. Houghton Mifflin, 1984.

Lowry, Lois. *Anastasia Krupnik*. Houghton Mifflin, 1979.

Lowry, Lois. *The Giver*. Houghton Mifflin, 1993.

Lowry, Lois. *Number The Stars*. Houghton Mifflin, 1989.

Lunn, Janet, ed. *The Unseen: Scary Stories*. Lester, 1994.

Mackay, Claire. *Laughs*. Tundra, 1997.

MacLachlan, Patricia. *Sarah, Plain and Tall*. HarperCollins, 1985.

MacLeod, Elizabeth. *Dinosaurs: The Fastest, the Fiercest, the Most Amazing*. Illustrated by Gordon Sauvé. Penguin, 1994.

Maestro, Marco and Giulio. *What Do You Hear When Cows Sing? And Other Silly Riddles* (An I Can Read Book). HarperCollins, 1996.

Maguire, Arlene. *Dinosaur Pop-up ABC*. Illustrated by Paul Mirocha. Simon & Schuster, 1995.

Marschall, Ken. *Inside the Titanic: A Giant Cutaway Book*. Little, Brown, 1997.

Martin, Jr., Bill. *Brown Bear, Brown Bear*. Holt, 1967.

Martin, Les. *Ghost in the Machine* (The X Files, #11). HarperCollins, 1997.

Martin, Terry. *Open House* (A Lift-the-Flap Book*)*. Illustrated by Steve Noon. Dorling Kindersley, 1996.

Maruki, Toshi. *Hiroshima No Pika*. Lothrop, Lee & Shepard, 1980.

Marzolla, Jean. *I Spy Super Challenger: A Book of Picture Riddles*. Photography by Walter Wick. Scholastic, 1997.

Mathers, Petra. *Lottie's New Beach Towel*. Atheneum, 1998.

Mayer, Mercer. *Frog Goes to Dinner*. Dial, 1974.

Maynard, Christopher. *Informania: Sharks*. Candlewick, 1997.

McCully, Emily A. *Picnic*. HarperCollins, 1984.

McCurdy, Michael, illus. *The Sailor's Alphabet*. Houghton Mifflin, 1998.

McGrath, Barbara. *The M&M's Counting Book*. Charlesbridge, 1994.

McFarlane, Brian. *Hockey for Kids: Heroes, Tips and Facts*. Kids Can, 1994/Beech Tree, 1996.

McKissack, Patricia C. *The Dark-Thirty: Southern Tales of the Supernatural*. Illustrated by Brian Pinkney. Knopf, 1992.

McMullan, K.H. *Dragon Slayers' Academy: The New Kid at School*. Illustrated by Bill Basso. Grosset & Dunlap, 1997.

McMullan, Kate. *The Frog Prince Drinks Diet Croak and other Wacky Fairy Tale Jokes*. Scholastic, 1997.

McNaughton, Colin. *Here Come The Aliens!* Candlewick, 1995.

Micklethwait, Lucy. *I Spy Two Eyes: Numbers in Art*. Greenwillow, 1993.

Miller, Jonathan. *The Human Body*. Designed by David Pelham. Viking, 1983.

Miller, Marvin. *Codemaster: Book 1*. Scholastic, 1998.

Mollel, Tolowa. M. *The Orphan Boy*. Illustrated by Paul Morin. Oxford, 1990.

Morimoto, Junko. *My Hiroshima*. Viking, 1987.

Morrison, Grant. *Batman Gothic*. Art by Klaus Johnson. DC Comics, 1992.

Moscovich, Ivan. *The Think Tank*. Dorling Kindersley. 1998.

Moss, Marissa. *My Notebook* (with *Help from Amelia*) by ____ and Marissa Moss. Tricycle Press, 1997.

Most, Bernard. *There's an Ant in Anthony*. Mulberry, 1992.

Mowat, Farley. *Lost in the Barrens*. McClelland & Stewart, 1973 & 1989/Little & Brown, 1956.

Mowat, Farley. *Owls in the Family*. Little Brown, 1961.

Munsch, Robert and Askar Saoussan. *From Far Away*. Illustrated by Michael Martchenko. Annick, 1995.

Munsch, Robert. *Good Families Don't*. Doubleday Canada, 1990.

Munsch, Robert. *Moira's Birthday*. Illustrated by Michael Martchenko. Annick, 1995.

Munsch, Robert. *Munschworks: The First Munsch Collection*. Illustrated by Michael Martchenko. Annick, 1998.

Munsch, Robert. *The Paper Bag Princess*. Illustrated by Michael Martchenko. Annick, 1980.

Munsch, Robert. *Pigs*. Illustrated by Michael Martchenko. Annick, 1989.

Munsch, Robert. *Stephanie's Ponytail*. Illustrated by Michael Martchenko. Annick, 1996.

Murphy, Stuart. *A Pair of Socks* (Mathstart). HarperCollins, 1996.

Napoli, Donna Jo. *The Prince of the Pond*. Illustrated by Judith Schachner. Puffin, 1994.

Naylor, Phyllis Reynolds. *Agony of Alice*. Atheneum, 1989.

Naylor, Phyllis Reynolds. *Shiloh*. Atheneum, 1991.

Naylor, Phyllis Reynolds. *Shiloh Season*. Atheneum, 1996.

Neuman, Marjorie. *Hornpipe's Hunt for Pirate Gold: A Puzzle Storybook*. Illustrated by Ben Cort. Candlewick, 1998.

Newfeld, Frank. *Creatures: An Alphabet for Adults and Worldly Children*. Groundwood, 1998.

Nilsen, Anna. *Terrormazia: A Hole New Kind of Maze Game*. Illustrated by Dom Mansell. Candlewick, 1995.

Novak, Matt. *Newt: The Antics of a Swamp Living Salamander* (An I Can Read Book). HarperCollins, 1996.

O'Brien, Eileen and Diana Riddell. *The Usborne Book of Secret Codes*. Illustrated by Mark Watkinson. Usborne, 1997.

O'Neill, Amanda. *Cats*. Kingfisher, 1998.

Oberman, Sheldon. *The Always Prayer Shawl*. Illustrated by Ted Lewin. Boyds Mills, 1994.

Octon, Henni and Elizabeth Honey. *45 + 47 Stella Street and Everything That Happened*. Annick, 1998.

Oppel, Kenneth. *Silverwing*. Simon & Schuster, 1997.

Orr, Richard. *Nature Cross-Sections*. Dorling Kindersley, 1995.

Osborne, Mary Pope. *Pirates Past Noon* (A Stepping Stone Book: Magic Tree House, #4). Random House, 1994.

*Our Changing Planet* (Voyages of Discovery). Scholastic, 1996.

Palatini, Margie. *Piggie Pie*. Illustrated by Howard Fine. Clarion, 1995.

Parish, Peggy. *Play Ball, Amelia Bedelia* (An I Can Read Book). Pictures by Wallace Tripp. HarperCollins, 1972.

Park, Barbara. *June B. Jones and Some Sneaky Peeky Spring* (A First Stepping Stone Book). Random House, 1994.

Park, Barbara. *Pssst! It's Me...the Bogeyman*. Illustrated by Stephen Kroninger. Atheneum, 1998.

Parker, Steve. *Making Tracks: Explore the World of Land Machines From Bikes to Bulldozers*. Candlewick, 1997.

Pascal, Francine. *No Escape!* (Sweet Valley Twins, #118). Bantam Doubleday Dell, 1998.

Paterson, Katherine. *The Great Gilly Hopkins*. HarperCollins, 1978.

Paulsen, Gary. *Amos Goes Bananas* (Culpepper Adventures). Delacorte, 1995.

Paulsen, Gary. *Brian's Winter*. Delacorte, 1996.

Paulsen, Gary. *Dogsong*. Bradbury, 1985.

Paulsen, Gary. *Hatchet*. Bradbury, 1987.

Paulsen, Gary. *My Life in Dog Years*. Delacorte, 1998.

Pearson, Kit. *This Land: A Cross-Country Anthology of Canadian Fiction for Young Readers*. Viking, 1998.

Peet, Bill. *Big Bad Bruce*. Houghton Mifflin, 1977.

Peet, Bill. *The Caboose Who Got Loose*. Houghton Mifflin, 1980.

Peet, Bill. *Chester the Worldly Pig*. Houghton Mifflin, 1978.

Peet, Bill. *Fly Homer Fly*. Houghton Mifflin, 1976.

Peet, Bill. *Pamela Camel*. Houghton Mifflin, 1984.

Peet, Bill. *Wump World*. Houghton Mifflin, 1981.

Pelham, David. *Sam's Pizza!* Dutton, 1996.

Pelham, David. *Say Cheese!* Dutton, 1998.

Pelham, David. *The Sensational Samburger*. Dutton, 1995.

Pepper, Dennis. *The Oxford Book of Scary Tales*. Oxford, 1992.

Perlman, Janet. *Cinderella Penguin or the Little Glass Flipper*. Kids Can, 1992.

Perret, Gene. *Super Funny School Jokes*. Illustrated by Stanford Hoffman. Sterling, 1991.

Pilkey, Dav. *The Adventures of Captain Underpants*. Blue Sky/Scholastic, 1997.

Pilkey, Dav. *The Silly Gooses*. Blue Sky/Scholastic, 1997.

Pinkwater, Daniel. *Mush: A Dog from Space*. Atheneum, 1995.

Piper, Watty. *The Little Engine That Could*. Illustrated by George and Doris Hauman. Platt & Munk, 1959.

Platt, Richard. *Stephen Biesty's Incredible Explosions: Exploded Views of Astonishing Things*. Illustrated by Stephen Biesty. Dorling Kindersley, 1996/Scholastic Canada, 1996.

Polacco, Patricia. *Chicken Sunday*. Philomel, 1992.

Polacco, Patricia. *The Keeping Quilt*. Simon & Schuster, 1988.

Polacco, Patricia. *Pink and Say*. Philomel, 1994.

Polacco, Patricia. *Rachenka's Eggs*. Philomel, 1988.

Polacco, Patricia. *Thank You, Mr. Falker*. Philomel, 1998.

Powling, Chris, ed. *The Kingfisher Book of Scary Stories*. Illustrated by Peter Bailey. Kingfisher, 1994.

Prelutsky, Jack, ed. *The Beauty of the Beast: Poems from the Animal Kingdom*. Illustrated by Meilo So. Knopf, 1997.

Prelutsky, Jack. *Dragons are Singing Tonight*. Illustrated by Peter Sis. Greenwillow, 1993.

Prelutsky, Jack, ed. *Imagine That: Poems of Never-Was*. Illustrated by Kevin Hawkes. Knopf, 1998.

Prelutsky, Jack. *The New Kid on the Block*. Illustrated by James Stevenson. Greenwillow, 1984.

Prelutsky, Jack. *Nightmares: Poems to Trouble Your Sleep*. Illustrated by Arnold Lobel. Greenwillow, 1976.

Prelutsky, Jack, ed. *The Random House Book of Poetry*. Illustrated by Arnold Lobel. Random House, 1983.

*Presenting Leptoceratops: Book, Bones, Egg and Poster*. A Sommerville House Book/Andrews & McMeel, 1991.

Priceman, Marjorie. *My Nine Lives by Clio*. Atheneum, 1998.

Pritchard, Louise. *My Pony*. Stoddart/Dorling Kindersley, 1998.

Pulleyn, Micah and Sarah Bracken. *Kids in the Kitchen: 100 Delicious, Fun and Healthy Recipes to Cook and Bake*. Sterling, 1995.

*Puzzle Gallery: Pets*. Knopf, 1997.

*Puzzles and Puzzlers*. By the editors of Owl Magazine. Greey de Pencier, 1987/ Firefly, 1987.

Reynolds, David West. *Star Wars: Incredible Cross-Sections*. Illustrated by Hans Jenssen and Richard Chasemore. Dorling Kindersley/Stoddart, 1998.

Reynolds, David West. *Star Wars: The Visual Dictionary*. Stoddart/Dorling Kindersley, 1998.

Richards, Jon. *Cutaway Racing Cars*. Copper Beech Books, 1998.

Risinger, Matt and Phillip Yates. *Great Book of Zany Jokes*. Illustrated by Lucy Corvino. Sterling, 1995.

Robertus, Polly. *The Dog Who Had Kittens*. Illustrated by Janet Stevens. Holiday House, 1988.

Robinson, Barbara. *The Best Christmas Pageant Ever*. HarperCollins, 1972.

Rogers, Paul. *What Can You See?* Illustrations by Kazuko. Bantam Doubleday Dell, 1998.

Rossiter, Sean. *Goal Scoring*. Douglas & McIntyre, 1997.

Rothaus, Jim. *Baseball Jokes*. Illustrated by Viki Woodworth. Childs World, 1996.

Royston, Angela. *Fire Fighter!* (Know It All Readers). Dorling Kindersley/Fenn, 1998.

Rubin, Jim. *Porkchop to the Rescue* (Doug Chronicles). Disney, 1998.

Rylant, Cynthia. *Henry and Mudge: The First Book*. Illustrated by Sucie Stevenson. Simon & Schuster, 1987.

Sabuda, Robert. *ABC Disney: An Alphabet Pop-up*. Disney, 1998.

Sackson, Sid. *The Book of Classic Board Games*. Klutz, 1991.

Sage, Allison, ed. *The Hutchinson Treasury of Children's Poetry*. Hutchinson, 1998.

Sage, James. *Sassy Gracie*. Illustrated by Pierre Pratt. Macmillan, 1998.

San Souci, Robert. *The Legend of Fa Mulan*. Illustrated by Jean and Mou-Sien Tseng. Hyperion, 1998.

San Souci, Robert. *More Short and Shivery: Thirty Terrifying Tales*. Illustrated by Katherine Coville and Jacqueline Rogers. Delacorte, 1996.

Sandved, Kjell B. *The Butterfly Alphabet*. Scholastic, 1996.

Saunders, Susan. *The Revenge of the Pirate Ghost* (The Black Cat Club: A Trophy Chapter Book). Illustrated by Jane Manning. HarperCollins, 1997.

Schnetzler, Pattie. *Ten Little Dinosaurs*. Illustrated by Jim Harris. Accord, 1996.

Schulman, Janet, ed. *20th Century Children's Book Treasury: Celebrated Picture Books and Stories to Read Aloud*. Knopf, 1998.

Schwartz, Alvin. *The Cat's Elbow and Other Secret Languages*. Illustrated by Margot Zemach. Farrar, Straus & Giroux, 1982.

Schwartz, Alvin. *Gold and Silver, Silver and Gold: Tales of Hidden Treasure*. Farrar Straus & Giroux, 1988.

Schwartz, Alvin. *Scary Stories to Tell in the Dark*. Illustrated by Stephen Gammell. HarperCollins, 1981.

Scieszka, Jon. *The Frog Prince*. Illustrated by Steve Johnson. Viking, 1994.

Scieszka, Jon. *Squids Will Be Squids: Fresh Morals, Beastly Fables*. Illustrated by Lane Smith. Viking, 1998.

Scieszka, Jon. *The True Story of the Three Little Pigs by A. Wolf*. Illustrated by Lane Smith. Viking, 1989.

Scieszka, Jon. *Tut, Tut* (The Time Warp Trio). Illustrated by Lane Smith. Viking, 1995.

*Scrabble Puzzles*. Warner, 1995.

Seuss, Dr. (with some help from Jack Prelutsky and Lane Smith). *Hurray for Diffendoofer Day!* Knopf, 1998.

Shannon, George. *Tomorrow's Alphabet*. Illustrated by Donald Crews. Greenwillow, 1996.

Sharmat, Marjorie Weinman. *Nate the Great and the Missing Key* (Nate the Great). Illustrated by Marc Simont. Bantam Doubleday Dell, 1982.

Shaw, Nancy. *Sheep in a Jeep*. Illustrated by Margot Apple. Houghton Mifflin, 1986.

Shea, George. *Amazing Rescues* (STEP into Reading). Illustrated by Marshall H. Peck III. Random House, 1992.

Shub, E. *The White Stallion*. Illustrated by Rachel Isadora. Bantam, 1982.

Silverstein, Shel. *Falling Up*. HarperCollins, 1996.

Silverstein, Shel. *Where the Sidewalk Ends*. HarperCollins, 1974.

Simon, Seymour. *The Halloween Horror and Other Cases* (Einstein Anderson Science Detective). Illustrated by S. D. Schindler. Morrow, 1997.

Skofield, James. *Detective Dinosaur Lost and Found* (An I Can Read Book). Pictures by R.W. Alley. HarperCollins, 1998.

Smith, Janice Lee. *Wizard and Wart in Trouble* (An I Can Read Book). Pictures by Paul Meisel. HarperCollins, 1998.

Smyth, Ian. *The Young Baseball Player: A Young Enthusiast's Guide to Baseball*. Stoddart/Dorling Kindersley, 1998.

Sobol, Donald. *Encyclopedia Brown Saves the Day*. Dutton, 1970.

Somerville, Louisa. *Rescue Vehicles* (Look Inside Cross-Sections). Illustrated by Hans Jenssen. Dorling Kindersley, 1995.

*Space Shuttle and Hubble Telescope: Cross-Section Puzzle*. Dorling Kindersley, 1997.

Sperry, Armstrong. *Call It Courage*. Macmillan, 1940.

Spiegelman, Art. *Maus, A Survivor's Tale: My Father Bleeds History*. Pantheon, 1973.

Spier, Peter. *Noah's Ark*. Doubleday, 1977.

Spier, Peter. *Peter Spier's Rain*. Doubleday, 1982.

Spirn, Michele Sobel. *The Know-Nothings* (An I Can Read Book). Pictures by R. W. Alley. HarperCollins, 1995.

Spurr, Elizabeth. *The Long, Long Letter*. Illustrated by David Catrow. Hyperion, 1997.

Steele, Philip. *Step into the Roman Empire*. Lorenz, 1997.

Steig, William. *Dominic*. Farrar, Straus & Giroux, 1972.

Steiner, Joan. *Look-Alikes: Discover a Land Where Things Are Not As They Appear*. Photography by Thomas Lindley. Little Brown, 1998.

Stott, Carole. *Night Sky* (Eyewitness Explorers). Dorling Kindersley/Stoddart, 1993.

Strasser, Todd. *Kids' Book of Gross Facts and Feats*. Watermill, 1998.

Stutson, Caroline. *By the Light of the Halloween Moon*. Illustrated by Kevin Hawkes. Penguin, 1993.

Sutton, Richard. *Car* (Eyewitness Books). Stoddart/ Dorling Kindersley, 1990.

Swanson, Diane. *Coyotes in the Crosswalk: Canadian Wildlife in the City*. Illustrated by Douglas Penhale. Voyageur, 1995.

Swanson, Diane. *A Toothy Tongue and One Long Foot: Nature Activities for Kids*. Whitecap, 1992.

Tallarico, Tony. *What's Wrong Here? At School*. Kidsbooks, 1998.

Tanaka, Shelley. *On Board the Titanic*. Illustrated by Ken Marschall. Scholastic Canada/Madison; Hyperion/Madison, 1997.

Tanaka, Shelley. *The Buried City of Pompeii: What It Was Like When Vesuvius Exploded*. Illustrated by Greg Ruhl. Scholastic Canada/Madison; Hyperion/ Madison, 1997.

Taylor, Barbara. *The Really Deadly and Dangerous Dinosaur: And Other Monsters of the Prehistoric World*. Stoddart/ Dorling Kindersley, 1997.

Taylor, David. *Nature's Creatures of the Dark: A Pop-up, Glow-in-the-Dark Exploration*. Dial, 1993.

Terban, Marvin. *Scholastic Dictionary of Idioms: More than 600 Phrases, Sayings and Expressions*. Scholastic, 1996.

Terban, Marvin. *Too Hot To Hoot: Funny Palindrome Riddles*. Illustrated by Giulio Maestro. Clarion, 1985.

Tolhurst, Marilyn. *Knights* (The Age of Adventure to Unlock and Discover). Running Press, 1995.

Tomb, Howard and Dennis Kunkel. *MicroAliens: Dazzling Journeys with an Electron Microscope*. Farrar, Straus & Giroux, 1993.

*Totally Amazing Spiders*. Golden Books, 1998.

Townsend, Charles. *World's Most Perplexing Puzzles*. Sterling, 1995.

Trelease, Jim, ed. *Hey! Listen to This: Stories to Read Aloud*. Penguin, 1992.

Turkle, Brinton. *Deep in the Forest*. Dutton, 1976.

Turnbull, Andy with Debora Pearson. *My Arctic Adventure: By Truck to the North*. Annick, 1998.

Tuxworth, Nicola. *Let's Look at Things That Go*. Lorenz, 1998.

Tuyen, P. D. *Classic Origami*. Sterling, 1995.

*Under the Sea* (Discovery Box). Scholastic, 1997.

Van Allsburg, Chris. *Jumanji*. Houghton Mifflin, 1981.

Van Allsburg, Chris. *Polar Express*. Houghton Mifflin, 1985.

Van Allsburg, Chris. *Two Bad Ants*. Houghton Mifflin, 1988.

Van Allsburg, Chris. *The Z was Zapped*. Houghton Mifflin, 1987.

van der Meer, Ron and Dr. Alan McGowan. *Sailing Ships*. Paintings by Borje Svensson. Viking, 1984.

Vaughan, Marcia. *Goldsworthy and Mort: In Spring Soup* (A Ready, Set, Read Book). Illustrated by Linda Hendry. HarperCollins, 1991.

Veitch, Tom. *Star Wars: Dark Empire II*. Illustrated by Cam Kennedy. Dark Horse Comics, 1995.

Viorst, Judith. *The 10th Good Thing About Barney*. Atheneum, 1971.

Viorst, Judith. *The Alphabet from Z to A, with Much Confusion on the Way*. Illustrated by R. Hull. Atheneum, 1994.

*The Visual Dictionary of Cars* (Eyewitness Visual Dictionaries). Stoddart/Dorling Kindersley, 1992.

Walker, S. *Heads and Tails*. Puffin, 1996.

Walton, Rick and Ann. *I Toad You So: Riddles About Frogs and Toads*. Pictures by Susan Slattery Burke. Lerner, 1991.

Warner, Gertrude Chandler. *The Firehouse Mystery* (The Box Car Children, #56). Illustrated by Charles Tang. Albert Whitman, 1997.

Waterton, Betty. *The Lighthouse Dog*. Illustrated by Dean Griffiths. Orca, 1997.

Watts, Barrie. *See How They Grow: Mouse*. Dorling Kindersley/Scholastic Canada, 1992.

Weber, Ken. *Five-Minute Mysteries*. Stoddart, 1994.

Wegman, William. *My Town*. Hyperion, 1998.

Weir, Joan. *Sky Lodge Mystery and Other Stories* (Mystery Club). Overlea, 1988.

Weitzman, Jacqueline Preiss. *You Can't Take a Balloon into the Metropolitan Museum*. Illustrated by Robin Preiss Glasser. Dial, 1998.

Whatley, Bruce and Rosie Smith. *Whatley's Quest*. Angus & Robertson/HarperCollins, 1994.

White, E.B. *Charlotte's Web*. Illustrated by Garth Williams. HarperCollins, 1952.

Whitman, John. *Star Wars: The Death Star*. Illustrated by Barbara Gibson. Little Brown, 1997.

Wiesner, David. *Tuesday*. Clarion, 1991.

Wilbur, Richard. *The Disappearing Alphabet*. Illustrated by David Diaz. Harcourt Brace, 1998.

Wilcox. Charlotte. *Mummies and Their Mysteries*. Carolrhoda, 1993.

Wild, Margaret. *The Very Best of Friends*. Illustrated by Julie Vivas. Harcourt Brace, 1990.

Wilder, Laura Ingalls. *My Little House Cookbook*. Recipes by Amy Cotler. Illustrated by Holly Jones. HarperCollins, 1996.

Wilkes, Angela. *The Children's Step-by-Step Book*. Macmillan Canada/Dorling Kindersley, 1994.

Wilkinson, Philip. *Spacebusters: The Race to the Moon* (Eyewitness Readers). Dorling Kindersley, 1998.

Williams, Helga. *Wordplay*. Illustrated by Colin William. Sono Nis Press, 1997.

Wilson, Anthony. *Visual Timeline of Transportation*. Dorling Kindersley, 1995.

Wilson, Eric. *Escape from Big Muddy*. HarperCollins, 1997.

Wilson, Eric. *Ghost of Lunenburg Manor*. Stoddart, 1993.

Winch, John. *The Old Woman Who Loved to Read*. Holiday House, 1996.

Windham, Ryder. *Star Wars: Battle of the Bounty Hunters*. Boxtree, 1996.

Winston, Mary, ed. *American Heart Association Kids' Cookbook*. Illustrated by Joan Holub. Times/Random House, 1993.

Wisniewski, David. *The Secret Knowledge of Grownups*. Lothrop, Lee & Shephard, 1998.

Wood, Audrey. *The Napping House Wakes Up*. Illustrated by Don Wood. Harcourt Brace, 1984/pop-up edition, 1994.

Wood, Jenny. *Jungles: Facts, Stories, Activities*. Scholastic, 1991.

*World Almanac for Kids 1999*. World Almanac Books, 1998.

Wright, Rachel. *The Viking News*. Candlewick, 1998.

Wyatt, Valerie. *The Science Book for Girls and Other Intelligent Beings*. Kids Can, 1993.

Yep, Laurence. *Later, Gator*. Hyperion, 1995.
Yolen, Jane. *Commander Toad and the Intergalactic Spy* (Commander Toad). Illustrated by Bruce Degen. Putnam, 1986.
Yolen, Jane. *The Girl Who Loved the Wind*. Illustrated by Ed Young. HarperCollins, 1972.
Young, Ed. *Cat and Rat: The Legend of the Chinese Zodiac*. Holt, 1995.
Young, Ed. *Lon Po Po: A Red Riding Hood Story from China*. Philomel, 1989.
Young, Ed. *Seven Blind Mice: An Indian Fable*. Philomel, 1992.
Young, Jay. *The Most Amazing Science Pop-up Book*. HarperCollins, 1994.

Zeman, Ludmila. *Gilgamesh the King*. Tundra, 1992.

# Non-print Titles

## CD-ROMs

*Beethoven Lives Upstairs*. BMG Interactive Entertainment, 1995.
*Castle Explorer*. Dorling Kindersley Multimedia, 1996.
*Earth Quest*. Dorling Kindersley Multimedia, 1997.
*Eyewitness Encyclopedia of Science*. Dorling Kindersley Multimedia, 1994.
*I Spy*. Scholastic, 1997.
*I Spy: Brain-Building Games for Kids!* Scholastic.
*The Magic School Bus Explores the Solar System*. Scholastic, 1996.
*Maurice Ashley Teaches Chess: For Beginners and Intermediate Players*. Simon & Schuster, 1995.
*The New Kid on the Block*. Based on the book by Jack Prelutsky. Broderbund Software, 1993.
*Northern Lights: The Soccer Trails*. Based on the book by Michael Kusugak. Discis Knowledge Research, 1994.
*Planet Dexter's Grossology: Gross Science That Kids Want to Learn!* Segasoft Networks, 1997.
Polar Express. Based on the book by Chris Van Allsburg. Houghton Mifflin Interactive, 1996.
*Starsites*. DNA Media, 1998.
*Stephen Biesty's Incredible Cross-Sections: Stowaway*. Dorling Kindersley, 1994.
*Super Solvers Gizmos and Gadgets!* The Learning Company, 1995.
*Up to the Himalayas*. DNA Media, 1998.
*The Way Things Work*. Based on the book by David Macaulay. Dorling Kindersley Multimedia, 1994.
*Where in the World is Carmen Sandiego?* Broderbund Software, 1996.

## Taped Books

Coville, Bruce. *The Ghost in the Big Brass Bed*. Read by Christina Moore. Recorded Books, 1996 (4.75 hours).
Cushman, Karen. *Catherine, Called Birdy*. Performance by Kate Maberly. Bantam Doubleday Dell Audio Publishing, 1996 (3 hours).
Dahl, Roald. *Matilda*. Read by Ron Keith. Recorded Books, 1994 (5.25 hours).

Fleishman, Paul. *Joyful Noise: Poems for Two Voices* (3 hours).
Hobbs, Will. *Beardance*. Narrated by George Guidall. Recorded Books (5.5 hours).
Jacques, Brian. *Red Wall*. Narrated by Ron Keith. Recorded Books, 1995 (13.25 hours).
Jacques, Brian. *Red Wall*. Performance with 23 voices by Brian Jacques. Listening Library, 1997 (11 hours).
O'Dell, Scott. *Island of the Blue Dolphins*. Performance by Tantoo Cardinal. Bantam Doubleday Dell Audio Publishing.
Paterson, Katherine. *Bridge to Terabithia*. Read by Tom Stechschulte. Recorded Books, 1997 (4 hours).
Paterson, Katherine. *The Great Gilly Hopkins*. Read by Alyssa Bresnahan. Recorded Books, 1996 (4.75 hours).
Paulsen, Gary. *Skydive* (The Gary Paulsen World of Adventure Fiction on Cassette Series). Narrated by Jeff Woodman. Recorded Books, 1996 (1 hour).
Taylor, Theodore. *The Cay*. Performance by Le Var Burton. BDD Audio Publishing, 1992 (1.75 hours).
Yolen, Jane. *Wizard's Hall*. Read by the author. Listening Library, 1995 (3 hours).

### Videos

*Amazing Grace*. Based on the book by Mary Hoffman. Weston Woods, 1995.
*The BFG*. Adapted by John Hambly. Based on the book by Roald Dahl. Thames Video, 1996.
*The Fool of the World and the Flying Ship*. Based on the book by Arthur Ransome. Cosgrove Hall and WGBH Boston, 1991.
*James and the Giant Peach*. Based on the book by Roald Dahl. 20th Century Fox Video/Walt Disney Pictures, 1996.
*Johann's Gift to Christmas*. Based on the book by Jack Richards. O'B & D Films in association with the Canadian Broadcasting Corporation, 1991.
*Linnea in Monet's Garden*. Based on the book by Leena Anderson and Christiana Bjork. First Run Features, 1994.
*The Mouse and the Motorcycle*. Based on the book by Beverly Cleary. Churchill Films, 1991.
*The Story of Rosy Dock*. Based on the book by Jeannie Baker. New Dimension Media, 1996.
*The Sweater*. Based on the book *The Hockey Sweater* by Roch Carrier. National Film Board of Canada, 1996.
*Where the Forest Meets the Sea*. Based on the book by Jeannie Baker. Spoken Arts, 1987.

## Professional Titles

Asher, Steven. "Topic Interest and Children's Reading Comprehension." In R. Spiro et al., eds., *Theoretical Issues in Reading Comprehension*. Hillsdale, NJ: Erlbaum, 1980.
Belloni, Loretta and Jongsma, Eugene. "The Effects of Interest on Reading Comprehension of Low-Achieving Students." *Journal of Reading*, 22, 1997, 106-109.
Brophy, Jere and Good, Thomas. "Teacher Communication of Differential

Expectations for Children's Classroom Performance: Some Behavioral Data." *Journal of Educational Psychology*, 61, 1970, 365-374.

Clay, Marie. *Becoming Literate: The Construction of Inner Control*. Portsmouth, NH: Heinemann, 1991.

Dayton-Sakari, Mary. "Reading Your Readers: The Observation of Ability and Control through Students' Nonverbal Communication." In M. Dayton-Sakari and C. Miller, eds., *Connections '96*. Victoria, BC: University of Victoria, 1996.

Dayton-Sakari, Mary. "Struggling Readers Don't Work at Reading: They Just Get Their Teacher To!" *Intervention in School and Clinic*, 32, (5), 1997, 295-301.

Department of Education and Science. *A Language for Life* (The Bullock Report). London, UK: Her Majesty's Stationery Office, 1975.

Dwyer, Edward and Evelyn. "How Teacher Attitudes Influence Reading Achievement." In E. H. Cramer and M. Castle, eds., *Fostering the Love of Reading: The Affective Domain in Reading Education*. Newark, DE: IRA, 1994.

Early, Margaret. "Using Key Visuals to Aid ESL Students' Text Comprehension." *Reading-Canada-Lecture*, 7, (4), 1989, 202-212.

Galloway, Charles. *Silent Language in the Classroom*. Bloomington, IN: Phi Delta Kappa, 1976.

Guthrie, Jean. "Effective Teaching Practices." *The Reading Teacher*, 35, 1982, 766-768.

Hiebert, Elfrieda. "Issues Related to Home Influences in Young Children's Print-Related Development." In D. B. Yaden and S. Templeton, eds., *Metalinguistic Awareness and Beginning Reading*. Portsmouth, NH: Heinemann, 1986.

Holdaway, Don. *The Foundations of Literacy*. Portsmouth, NH: Heinemann, 1979.

Huck, Charlotte. *Children's Literature in the Elementary School*. Madison, WI: Brown & Benchmark, 1996.

Irvine, Joan. *How To Make Pop-ups!* Illustrated by Barbara Reid. Toronto, ON: Kids Can Press, 1987.

Jobe, Ron. *Cultural Connections*. Markham, ON: Pembroke, 1993.

Johns, Jerry. "The Effect of Self-Selection, Interest and Motivation upon Independent, Instructional and Frustrational Levels." *The Reading Teacher*, 50, (4), 1997, 278-282.

Little, Jean. *Little by Little: A Writer's Education*. Viking, 1987.

Martin Jr. Bill. *Sounds of Language*. Allen, TX: DLM, 1991 (Reading Series, grades 1–6 teachers' manual, 74-91).

McCornick, Sandra. *Instructing Students Who Have Literacy Problems*. Englewood Cliffs, NJ: Merril, 1995.

National Assessment of Educational Progress. *Reading Comprehension of American Youth: Do They Understand What They Read?* Report No. 11-R-02. Denver CO: Education Commission of the United States, 1982.

Pappas, Christine, Kiefer, Barbara and Levstik, Linda. *An Integrated Language Perspective in the Elementary School*. NY: Longman, 1995.

Rosenthal, Robert and Jacobson, Lonore. *Pygmalion in the Classroom*. NY: Holt, Rinehart & Winston, 1968.

Spinelli, J. *Knots in My Yo-Yo String: The Autobiography of a Kid*. NY: Knopf, 1998.

Stauffer, Russell, ed. *The First Grade Reading Studies: Findings of Individual Investigations*. Newark, DE: IRA, 1967.

Temple, Charles and Gillet, Jean. *Language and Literacy: A Lively Approach*. NY: HarperCollins, 1996.

Thomas, Karen. "Early Reading as a Social Interaction Process." *Language Arts*, 62, 1985, 469-475.

Trelease, Jim. *The New Read-Aloud Handbook*. NY: Penguin, 1991.

Vaughn, Joseph. "The Effect of Interest on Reading Comprehension among Ability Groups and across Grade Levels." In G.H. McNinch & W.D. Miller, eds., *Reading: Convention and Inquiry*. Clemson, SC: National Reading Conference, 1975.

Wang, Margaret. "Development and Consequences of Students' Sense of Personal Control." In J. M. Levine and M.C. Wang, eds., *Teacher and Student Perceptions: Implications for Learning*. Hillsdale, NJ: Erlbaum, 1983.

Worthy, Jo. "Removing Barriers to Voluntary Reading for Reluctant Readers: The Role of School and Classroom Libraries." *Language Arts*, 73, 1996, 483-492.